FROM
THE BOX
TO THE
MOUNTAINTOP

The Journey To Heal My Soul

Matthew J. Newland

Author's Note: This memoir recounts the author's personal experiences with trauma and healing. While the events described are true to the author's memory and experience, some names have been changed to protect the privacy of the individuals who helped in my healing journey.

Warning: This book contains descriptions of sexual abuse, trauma, and suicidal ideation. Reader discretion is advised.

Crisis Resources: If you are experiencing suicidal thoughts, please call or text 988 for immediate help.

Paperback ISBN: 979-8-9995128-0-2
eBook ISBN: 979-8-9995128-1-9

First Edition

Printed in the United States of America

To my children - you are loved exactly as you are.

CONTENTS

Chapter 1

THE BEGINNING

INTRO

Healing my soul - wow, the title sounds like a hefty topic. Almost like a 'How To' book! How to heal my soul! Or maybe your soul? I didn't intend to head out on this journey to heal my soul. But, here I am. Here we are.

One of many things I've learned on this journey is that nothing went as expected. I learned to cry. Yup, true story. I thought I was incapable of crying at different points in my life. My emotions were so stoic - I knew something was wrong with me. Why couldn't I cry? I also found great humor in the darkest of places.

Another thing I've learned is that I'm not the only one on a journey. Everyone is. My journey is full of wonderful and unique characters, some of whom helped me along my way and others who caused great pain.

The trouble with sharing this journey as I'm starting to do now, is where to start and how to share some of the darkest corners of my memories in a way that doesn't cause you, the reader, pain. The goal is to give you insight. Without darkness there is no light. To know that you can succeed is to know failure. Failure is our greatest teacher.

Sure, you may cry if something hits you just right. I mean, I did while writing this. For some sections of this book, I relived things I wished to forget and maybe you'll feel the pain I was in when it happened.

I have found that in my darkest moments, laughter has been and continues to be the best path forward for me. I've got a quirky sense of humor. Kind of dry, not biting, self-deprecating at times, but like an exclamation point! There is absurdity in everyday life. I like to point it out.

So, why am I sharing my story? Because, I hope reading about what I went through may help you on your journey. My truth may shed some light that helps you with your own truth.

This journey would take me from a soccer injury in 2008, through two years of chronic pain and physical therapy, to a near suicide attempt in July 2010, and finally to understanding what had been haunting me all along.

Well, that's the intro...hang on tight! This may well be a strange, painful, fulfilling, tragic and dare I say funny journey. How can it not be? There is no manual for how to heal your soul.

SOCCER

In the early 2000's, here I am in my 30's, average dad, trying to find ways to keep my kids active and enjoying their lives! You know, like all of us, I wanted their lives to be better than I had it growing up. And nothing says 'dad commitment' more than soccer!

I was late to signing my sons up for Concord's recreational soccer. I asked if there was any way we could make an arrangement so they could play. They said, "Yes, if you coach, we can put your son on your team."

That mishap became fifteen plus years of coaching indoor and outdoor recreational soccer - one of the most rewarding things I've done with my two boys. And more importantly, it put me in a position to keep my kids safe and keep all the kids on my team safe. Safe from what? Well, that's a story that wouldn't surface until much later...

So, when you coach soccer for years, sometimes you need to figure out if you can actually *play* the sport. Maybe need is too strong a word. But, I knew the rules and I wanted to see if that knowledge would translate! I joined both indoor and outdoor recreational soccer teams to show off my skills.

Skills? Oh, did I forget to mention I'd never actually played soccer before? I didn't know a thing about soccer before I dove in to coaching.

Sometimes, you're a much better soccer player in your head than your body is capable of actually performing on the pitch (field). I was and likely still am the greatest soccer player that has never actually played soccer in my head. My skills are legendary! Yes, you can laugh freely at that one!

In 2008, when I was 40 years old and had the shirt to prove it (#40)! I didn't buy a sports car for my midlife crisis, but I was determined to be a soccer star in the recreational league!

Hold up! Before I tell you what happened to me - I want to share that even with my skills (ha), I found myself playing for the A Division indoor soccer league. This is the top recreational league. This is where you play if you actually played on a real team at some point in your life and you were well above average.

It is worth repeating, I was playing with honest to goodness real soccer players who played real soccer. They were Scottish, Brazilian, and Argentinian. And we won the division! I was an A division indoor soccer league champion!

What I don't normally share in that story, is that I spent most of the time on the bench during the playoffs and only went in when my pro teammates got too winded to continue. My role was to give them rest! But the kids that I coached only knew what they saw, which was my team picture on the Wall of Champions! I was a great coach because I was a proven champion!

One night, while I was playing during a game of indoor soccer, I was launched into the boards (think hockey rink) in what, if filmed, would have made a funniest home videos segment somewhere. You know the one, where the guy is running and goes off course and backs into a wall and everyone covers their eyes with their hands, and looks between their fingers to see what happened? That was me. I was in significant back pain. I thought I bruised something - it hurt!

The next day, we were playing outdoor soccer in the adult recreation league. I had a sore back and even less skill than I had the day before, but I wasn't going to admit that.

I was defending. I moved left, then right and the ball went behind me. I stopped suddenly and pushed myself backward to get to the ball. My calf muscle ruptured and down I went. My illustrious soccer career came to a sudden and unexpected end despite all my impressively great skill. Yes, I'm still laughing at myself. You can too! It's okay!

I was helped off the field by a couple of teammates and then I was brought to urgent care. After a full exam, the doc concluded that I had in fact partially ruptured my calf muscle. I received an air cast, medications, instructions and a follow-up with orthopedics.

When I got to orthopedics they were examining my calf muscle to confirm the findings from urgent care. As he lifted my leg to see the movement of the calf muscle, I started to yelp from the pain and pleaded for the doctor to check my back.

My back! The pain was brutal. The doctor was surprised. I was there for my calf muscle. But, with my reaction to the pain he quickly got some imaging done, a further exam and so forth.

By the time I left that appointment, I was diagnosed with a partially ruptured calf muscle and three broken transverse process bones in my back. I was put in a back brace, given crutches, sent home, medicated for pain and told to see a physical therapist once the acute phase ended. This was the beginning of my pain. It would be years until I was diagnosed with PTSD.

About a year after my back injury, one of the back doctors I had seen over many months made a comment to me that I still remember to this day. I didn't understand it at the time. I mean, I didn't know I had PTSD so it didn't make sense. He said, after a follow-up exam of my back and seeing my anxiety about the pain, "You need to deal with whatever it is you're not dealing with. It is getting in the way of your back healing."

I didn't appreciate the insight at the time. I was mad at him for saying it. I was in brutal pain and he was talking about what? Something imaginary?

MARK, PHYSICAL THERAPIST #1

I went to my first physical therapy appointment and the PT wasn't a good fit. But, I observed another PT, who I'll call Mark, working, who seemed to have a good sense of humor. So, I switched to him. He called me Matty. He had a very deep voice that traveled throughout the clinic. We were about to start a friendship that neither of us knew was coming.

By now, I had some more information about my back and new issues surrounding my leg. In layman's terms, I had a nerve issue in my left leg that was causing my leg to give out at random times, I had transverse process issues, deteriorated discs (both in the lumbar region), sciatica and muscle atrophy in my leg and a whole host of tight muscles in my lower back that were causing significant pain whenever I moved.

By now, I was in chronic pain mode. Chronic pain does a number on your mind. It's a huge weight to know or believe you'll *never* be out of pain. You know that physical therapy is supposed to help, but when? How long will it take?

What I began to learn as I went to physical therapy, is that simply by going, I was taking action. Taking action means I had a chance to get better. Imagine being in constant pain for months and months and not doing anything to get better. Suicidal ideations could easily occur. The brain could believe or convince you that there is no hope.

As we went through the physical therapy process, we were a team. Mark was my coach, my cheerleader and quite often my comedian. I recall one day, trying to walk without crutches or a cane when I struggled to get up from the waiting room chair. Mark watched me intently, didn't offer to help, and patiently waited.

I know Mark was watching to see my gait and mobility. He was letting me get up on my own, which is a big deal for the mind and motivation. And he waited because, well, he had to. I was moving pretty slow.

So, once we started across the treatment and gym area, Mark said, "Let's go, Ninety." I replied, "Why are you calling me Ninety?" He laughed and said, "Cause you're moving around like you're ninety years old! Let's get going, Matty!" We both laughed.

This is the friendship we built. Support, humor and at times anger. That anger usually came from me. I'd get mad because I was in pain and he couldn't perfectly empathize. Mark would say, "You know I can't see your pain, right?"

That's the thing, you can't *see* someone's pain. Pain is such a unique and individual thing. I could see a wound on your leg and with empathy understand that you are in pain, "Man that wound looks brutal! I bet that hurts a lot." But, I can't see the pain. And I had no visible wounds. This becomes even more important when we talk about healing wounds in one's soul.

The more Mark worked on me, the more other symptoms would appear. Asthma attacks, hyperventilating, dizziness, and several times, I just passed out. This was a lot for any PT to deal with. I was so fortunate Mark was my physical therapist.

I was struggling in my head about giving up and there were times I was afraid he'd quit on me. We'd talk about that. Mark gave me his word he would never quit on me. We committed to each other that we were going to cross the finish line together.

There were times where Mark would suggest I see a specialist to get another opinion. But I was resistant. I always believed he was doing that to get rid of me. I knew as a patient I was a lot to deal with.

I can look back now and realize he was just trying to help me. He wasn't trying to get rid of me, but rather to help me find solutions to get me on the best path for my physical conditions.

By the time we finished physical therapy together, I had seen him for 134 visits over years. Mark never quit on me. No matter how many times, I hyperventilated, had a panic attack or passed out, he kept his word.

During one stretch we added another PT to the mix who worked in the town of Bedford. This arrangement was at the suggestion of a surgeon who also worked in the Bedford location. So, I'd go see this new physical therapist Monday, Wednesday and Friday for a specific form of physical therapy with gym equipment. On Tuesday and Thursday, I'd return to Mark and we'd do pool physical therapy. I would joke that I was doing PT, "Three if by land and two if by sea,"; "Surf and Turf"; "Pain and Pool" etc.

The pool therapy was especially key at the time, since it was a respite from the pain caused by the gym the day before. Being in the water softened the pain in the movements needed to loosen my muscles. The water resistance allowed me to 'weigh less' as I moved. And the resistance the water provided increased muscle strength. I'm a huge believer in the idea that "A body in motion, stays in motion."

So, one time while at the Bedford physical therapy location, I passed out while working with him. The doctor there was, what can I say, an asshole. Probably the only medical provider I'd describe that way during my entire healing journey. He clearly had a God complex. He knew everything and everyone was beneath him. He was a medical genius in his own head. He also wanted to be called "Doctor" - I'll get to that topic soon. You know, the kind of guy who wants it known that he is above you and you are less than.

He actually told me that his prescribed form of physical therapy wasn't working because I didn't believe in it or I hadn't tried hard enough. In my mind, passing out from pain while doing his form of physical therapy was probably an indication that there's a problem with his program. But, I'm sure his ego had no room for constructive feedback. Did I mention he was an asshole?

I got to my car after the appointment and called Mark. I was very upset, I told him the doctor quit on me. "I am never gonna heal! Why am I putting in all this effort?" He replied, "Matty, I'm not quitting on you. Get back up here and we will create a new plan."

I did what Mark said. We continued on, and we crossed the finish line together. I had made the progress I needed. My physical health improved.

Pain decreased. And to this day, we remain friends. Mark has his own practice now in Manchester.

I would be remiss if I didn't mention another physical therapist, an intern, who was working under him. He was a great guy too. We learned a lot from each other. I still stay in contact with him as well!

I also was fortunate enough to be on the Community Colleges of NH Foundation while the intern was working on his degree at the community college in Claremont, NH. This gave me an opportunity to go speak to his physical therapy class about my experiences with pain and to thank him in front of all his peers for the hard work he poured into me.

Even though I had improved quite a bit, by July of 2010, after nearly two years of chronic pain and struggling through physical therapy, I had reached my breaking point.

What I learned

Red flags I learned to watch for in any healthcare setting:

- *Providers who won't listen to your concerns or dismiss your symptoms*
- *Anyone who makes you feel rushed or like you're taking up too much time*
- *Practitioners who won't adjust their approach when something isn't working*
- *Medical staff who don't communicate with your other providers*
- *Anyone who makes you feel ashamed about your conditions or reactions*

Green flags that Mark showed: he kept his word, he communicated with my other doctors, he never made me feel like my reactions were "too much," and he celebrated my progress with me.

Chapter 2

THE CRISIS

EMOTIONAL PAIN EMERGES

Ah, so life is good! I made it through 134 visits of PT and I'm doing great! Well, not exactly great. I was a lot better for sure! But, I was still struggling. I got a respite from my back pain, but something was still off. There was a lingering pain. A deep pain. A pain that had not been treated yet.

I mentioned physical pain earlier as a trigger. But, what about emotional pain?

How do you rate emotional pain on the pain scale? In my case, my brain did it for me. As you'll soon read, when I was coming home from Acadia National Park I was planning to die by suicide That was my ten. Well, maybe an eleven…

My brain knew that I was holding in memories I couldn't handle. Memories so horrific and dark that my brain knew the only option I had to protect myself from that pain was death by suicide. Shut off the brain permanently, and I'll never have to relive the things that up until now, up until certain experiences with pain and my body in physical therapy, I had been able to 'forget' about. Not in the literal sense, I knew they were there. But, those memories were locked in THE BOX.

For decades, my mind had protected me from the contents in THE BOX. Constantly expending energy to keep an eye on THE BOX to ensure it never was opened. Spending a huge amount of mental energy to stifle anything I might see, feel, smell or taste that would reconnect me to THE BOX.

The brain is complex and powerful. Its solution to protect me from THE BOX was to shut off my ability to feel. I became stoic. No major highs or deep lows.

That doesn't mean I didn't laugh, get angry or get sad. It does mean, when I laughed, I knew something was funny - but I didn't feel it like others. And when I was sad, I rarely if ever cried. I remember wondering if I even knew how to cry at different points in my life.

I like to explain losing your ability to feel emotions this way. If you and I both held an ice cube in our hands - You would <u>feel</u> that the ice cube is cold - I would <u>know</u> that it is cold - It is a distinction with a huge difference as it relates to trauma.

That chronic physical pain from my soccer injuries wore down my mind until it could no longer protect me from THE BOX. My brain knew what was in THE BOX. My brain knew I couldn't handle the contents of THE BOX.

So, my brain, on the way home from Acadia National Park, devised a plan to die by suicide. I would execute the plan when I arrived home after everyone was asleep. The pain, both physical and emotional, would finally come to an end. My brain, somehow logically, convinced me this was the best and only solution.

It wasn't. And again, if you're thinking about suicide, it is not the right solution for you either. There are always options! That night in July 2010 became my rock bottom – and paradoxically, the beginning of my healing journey.

SUICIDAL/ACADIA

In July of 2010, I was driving home with my family from Acadia National Park, one of our favorite family vacation spots. As is the case in many families with young children and spouses, we all had differing timings for when the moment strikes! "I have to pee!" So, with frequent bathroom stops and meals, coming home from Acadia to our home in New Hampshire turned into more than a six-hour drive.

That is plenty of time to contemplate how to end your life. Yup - death by suicide!

As I will say many times throughout this book, if you are having suicidal thoughts, tell someone! Talk to a friend, go hang out with people, or call 988! They have great people there who can help you make sense of how you are feeling.

And if someone tells you they are suicidal, take it seriously, listen to them and ask them if they have a plan and if so what the plan is, the timetable and again, stay with them, love them and also call 988. These people can help!

Back to coming home from Acadia.

I found myself stuck in my head, trying to figure out how to end the pain I was in.

PLANS GO
AWRY

My plan to die by suicide was simple enough. Lock myself in the shed so my family wouldn't be the first to find me and take a lot of meds. My family would be protected from the trauma of finding my body and I was sure there was enough meds in the cabinet to stop my heart.

Frankly, it was a really really bad plan. I likely wouldn't have died and I would have been physically maimed forever, with organ damage and in more physical pain than I was currently in with my back. Imagine how much worse life would be if I had done it and ended up in more pain and in a worse condition that I was currently in? Not to mention the impacts on my family and friends.

When we got home, we started unpacking the car. My mind was racing. I wasn't able to think straight. I began to shake uncontrollably. I sat down at the kitchen table and rocked back and forth. My wife called a friend of ours who worked at the hospital and he came over. She assumed my back issues were the source of my conditions.

He asked me if I had taken any medications. He assumed the chronic back pain may have gotten to me and I may have inadvertently overdosed. I shook my head no. But, how did he know that was my plan, I wondered? He suggested we go to the hospital ER to have them look at my back. I agreed.

On the way, he told me he had to stop at his house first. Likely to let his spouse know he was going to be longer than expected. I waited in the car, still shaking uncontrollably. I didn't understand what was happening to me. Is this what a nervous breakdown feels like? Has my body given up due to the chronic pain?

When he returned to the car, I was laying sideways in the front seat, still shaking. He put his hand on my shoulder and asked me a question. I don't remember the question. But, I responded with, "I was planning my suicide." He listened and didn't respond. When we got to the ER, they got us in quickly; they knew who he was so I'm sure that helped.

They had my back pain history and decided I should have a spinal tap. For those who have had a spinal tap you'll know what I mean when I say - I had the worst headache after that I've ever had at that time in my life. More pain...pure pain.

Before the doc came back in, my friend pleaded with me to the point of crying himself for me to share with the doctor that I was suicidal with a plan. I remember thinking that I had never seen him cry before. I was too numb to realize what was happening.

I simply said to him, "you care about me." He grabbed my hand and said, "Please tell the doctor and don't negotiate your way out of this." It felt like my mind was exploding in both physical and emotional pain.

Whatever was in THE BOX I mentioned earlier - I was not able to keep it hidden or shut anymore. I knew that when THE BOX opened, my life as I knew it would be over. The only option I could think of was to die by suicide to stop the physical pain I was in and the more severe pain that THE BOX was about to unleash on me. It had to stay closed!

When the doctor returned, he talked about the results of the spinal tap. And some other imaging they had done. He asked me if I had any questions. And I replied, "No. But, I'm suicidal and I have a plan." Yup, I listened to my friend in that moment, and it changed my life.

That led to a psychologist coming in and telling me I needed to voluntarily admit myself to the behavioral health ward at Concord Hospital or I'd be involuntarily admitted to the state hospital for my own protection.

I agreed to voluntarily admit myself. After about a total of twenty-four hours in the ER they found a room for me in 5 West. That's the name of their behavioral health section in the hospital. Once I was admitted to 5

West, my friend went home. Now, I was on my own trying to keep THE BOX locked up and hidden from everyone. Especially myself.

Unfortunately, that friend and I were never able to get back on track after that night. I reached out to him a few times after I was healthy. But, I'm sure he was on his own journey and he needed to take a different road. That happens in life. We all have people in our lives for periods of time (seasons) that sometimes move on. It's okay, just a part of all our journeys.

But, if he is reading this book - feel free to reach out anytime. I'd love to hear from you. That night in July 2010 would become the turning point that led to my formal PTSD diagnosis just one month later.

5 WEST

While being admitted to 5 West, I had to give up everything. My phone, shoelaces, and ID. Everything. They locked it all away. The room I was in was dark. I couldn't move much because of the back pain and I couldn't sit up because of the spinal tap headache that followed.

Think of a spinal tap like this; they suck fluid out of your spine with a very large needle. That loss of fluid creates a bubble of air in the empty space in your spine. If you lie down and stay still, the bubble doesn't move. But, if you sit or stand up the bubble of air rises fast and slams against the base of your brain. The absolute worst headache I'd ever had at that point in my life.

The medical staff thought I was being disruptive and using the spinal headache as an excuse not to participate in their treatment plans for me. After a spinal doctor checked me over, he told the folks at 5 West that the symptoms were real and would last a few days while my body replenished the fluid that was removed. After a few days I was beginning to get around in less pain.

I met a person there I'll call Joyce. I think she was a psychologist. She passed away recently. The first day I met her, I was sitting in her office. She asked me some questions that were easy to answer. Then she said, "Why are you so anxious?"

"I'm not anxious," I defensively and instantly replied.

She said, "Oh, your bouncing leg seems to indicate that you are anxious."

"That? I've been bouncing my leg my whole life," I retorted, like that explained everything.

I thought, you know, I'm hyperactive. Maybe too much caffeine. But anxious? Come on?!? Really? Then she said the thing I've never forgotten. She said it matter of factly and without judgement or pity. She said, "You've been bouncing your leg your whole life? Matt, you've been anxious a very long time. Maybe we could talk about that?"

That is the moment I point to as the start of my recovery from the worst pain in my life - the contents of THE BOX.

THE BOX is where you hide the darkest moments of your life. We all have a box. Things we want to forget. Things our brains helps us pretend never happened. We think we can keep it closed.

The start of my journey to heal my soul. That was the first time it ever crossed my mind that maybe someone could help me. As I sit here typing this, I can't recall if Joyce and I talked about anything related to THE BOX. But, I knew THE BOX was opening and I couldn't keep it closed anymore.

Before I was discharged, I was told I needed to have three or four people on an emergency list that would agree to take my calls 24/7 in case I was suicidal again. My friends that I reached out to readily agreed. I was and still am fortunate to have such good friends.

I was placed on short term disability from work. I ended up being out of work for six months. I was told I should spend as much time as possible in nature. Walks in the woods. Sit on a bench and soak in the sounds, sights and smells. Listen to the birds. Pay attention to the smells of nature. Watch a sunset. I was given more psych meds than I thought anyone could possibly handle.

What I Learned

What I learned about inpatient psychiatric care:

- *Bring an advocate if possible - someone who can speak for you when you can't*
- *Ask questions about medications and their side effects*
- *Participate in treatment planning when you're able*
- *It's okay to feel scared or confused that's normal*
- *Take advantage of any therapy or groups offered, even if you don't feel like it*
- *Recovery isn't linear - some days will be worse than others*

Joyce asking about my leg bouncing was the first time someone helped me connect my physical symptoms to anxiety. Sometimes the smallest observations can be the biggest breakthroughs.

What I Learned

What I learned about psychiatric medications:

- *It often takes time to find the right combination - be patient with the process*
- *Keep a mood/symptom journal to track what's working and what isn't*
- *Don't stop medications suddenly - always work with your doctor to taper off safely*
- *Side effects are real and should be discussed honestly with your prescriber*
- *Some medications work better for some people than others - it's very individual*
- *Medication can be a tool to help you do the therapy work, not a cure by itself*
- *Don't let anyone shame you for taking or not taking medication - it's your choice*
- *Keep a list of medications you've tried and their effects – this becomes valuable when seeing new providers*

The "gray world" I experienced when my emotions were numbed by medication taught me that finding the right balance is crucial.

Chapter 3

DIAGNOSIS AND DISCOVERY

PTSD
DIAGNOSIS

Let's jump right in! On August 3, 2010, I was formally diagnosed with Post Traumatic Stress Disorder. I celebrate August 3rd every year. No, I don't actually host a party or anything. But I make a note of it. This is the date I've chosen to remember in the course of trying to heal my soul. It was on this date that I see myself finally recognizing I needed help.

There are a lot of places you can read about PTSD. So, I'm not going to pretend I'm any great new source of understanding, enlightenment or that I know how to diagnose PTSD or even which version I have.

According to some there are two types: PTSD vs. C-PTSD.

Both PTSD and C-PTSD result from the experience of something deeply traumatic and can cause flashbacks, nightmares, and insomnia. Both conditions can also make you feel intensely afraid and unsafe even though the danger has passed. However, despite these similarities, there are characteristics that differentiate C-PTSD from PTSD according to some experts.

The main difference between the two disorders is the frequency of the trauma. While PTSD can be caused by a single traumatic event that is of time limited duration, C-PTSD (Complex) on the other hand is caused by long-lasting trauma that continues or repeats for months or years at a time.

In my case, I've learned that I likely have Complex Post Traumatic Stress Disorder. Why? Well, keep reading and it will all make sense.

I may use the terms interchangeably as we go. I think the medical community is still debating adding CPTSD as an official diagnosis. They can debate that. To those of us that have either one, it doesn't matter what they call it. It sucks to have it. But, it can become a back burner issue over time and not run your life. Oh, PTSD will still be there, but as you heal it will not hold as much power over you.

If you choose to read this book, you probably have at least a general understanding about PTSD. What I've found living with PTSD is that though there are similarities in the general categories of PTSD what triggers the symptoms can be as unique as people are.

I'm no doctor or psychologist, but I was diagnosed with PTSD. I didn't read about PTSD in a college textbook and discuss it amongst intellectuals - I've got the inside scoop. I'm living with it! PTSD is the reason I met Steve...

STEVE, PSYCHOLOGIST

Steve has been my psychologist for well over a decade. He was and is the person who gets me and understands how I think. He knows me so well now, I trust him with anything. He has been consistent, compassionate, understanding and someone who can, without creating conflict, challenge me and my own thinking. He finds ways to get me to grow beyond my own limitations and step through the fear that holds me back at times.

I know that he always has my best interest at heart. In fact, I've told him that once he retires, he and I are going to be fast friends. Until then, he keeps the appropriate boundaries one should have between patient and therapist.

But, that comfort with Steve is not how things started. My journey with Steve was fraught, chaotic, and at times life-threatening. No, no, no. Steve never threatened my life! I handled that all on my own!

When I started with Steve, I couldn't speak. I'd sit there for an hour fearing THE BOX. What Box? We will get into that later. Hang in there!

My whole life would change if I allowed myself to look into THE BOX, and talking about it would make those things real all over again. So, I was paralyzed at the mere thought of opening THE BOX.

As we began therapy, Steve set things up to build trust between us. He didn't have me do anything hard in the beginning. Early on, each time he wanted to see if I was ready to talk, he'd ask a broad question and I'd withdraw. I wasn't ready.

Concurrently, another doctor who was managing my psych meds kept making changes. The idea is that we would find the right combination of meds that would bring me enough stability so that the trauma locked inside THE BOX would not throw me off when opened, so that I could begin to deal with it. As those changes were made, my world became colorless. Everything was gray. Nothing was bright. My emotions were even more stoic. No highs, no lows. Just one emotion. No happy, no sad.

As the medication swings settled down, I began to talk with Steve generally about THE BOX. I probably didn't refer to it as a box at the time. But, it makes sense to me now to describe it that way.

I'd describe to Steve what it felt like to have a BOX. I would tell him why I didn't want to open it. How I thought if I said out loud what was in THE BOX, my life would change forever. That box was the one thing keeping me safe from what was inside. Why would anyone want to open THE BOX?

As we began to discuss things relevant to THE BOX, I began to understand what was happening to my mind. I had brain pain. Brain Pain is what I call it when you are so emotionally distraught you can't mentally process anything. I also use brain pain to describe when suicidal ideations happen. It's the brain's way of letting you know it's hurting and needs help. No different than any other part of your body. We just can't see brain pain like we can a broken arm.

There is so much Steve and I discussed over the last decade, I can't possibly put it all in this book. But, what I can say is having someone like Steve on your journey of healing is exceptionally helpful. Steve has been my guide as I climbed the mountain. He's shared with me what to look out for, how to understand the terrain as I reached challenging paths, and reassured me when I doubted myself. He was my cheerleader when I crossed a ravine. He was my coach when I doubted which direction I should take. Oh and we also laughed. We laughed a lot.

Speaking of laughing, we still laugh about this. During this organized chaos of a journey, I "fired" Steve five or more times. I'd get mad about something and I'd "fire" him so he knew I was mad. It didn't matter that Steve had done nothing wrong...

On one occasion I went to his office and he pulled some psych jujitsu on me. I sat down angry and said, "Before I fire you, I want to know why you didn't call me!" Without missing a beat he replied, "I'm curious Matt, why were you calling?" And the next thing I know we are talking about me and my needs. My anger got sidetracked and by the time I left that appointment, I had forgotten I was even angry. Steve is awesome! Today we laugh about how many times I "fired" him.

I look back at those conversations fondly. Steve's a good dude. He always knew when to push me, congratulate me, be a cheerleader, when to be a support and when to encourage me to be brave.   The point here is that when you are faced with trauma on your journey, it may be a great help to you to find a guide who can help you make sense of the things that are overwhelming you.

Over the years Steve and I worked together, we met a lot. I had to have a schedule, of course. That was a big thing for me to feel safe. We would meet on, say, every Monday at 5:00 pm.

Over time Steve and I manipulated the regular schedule on occasion. Sometimes we'd try every two weeks as I got healthier. I hope you can understand how scary that was for me. If I had nightmares or worse, night terrors, it could be fourteen nights before I saw him again. How could I manage that long?!?

Each shift in schedule was sort of a milestone for me. It meant that I was making progress. And the medical provider who had been with me on my journey the longest, who I had spent the most time with, also believed I was getting healthier and thought I could handle the change.

No milestone was bigger than the one where we both concluded that I no longer needed a regular schedule. Yup, we eventually cut the schedule cord. I could still call Steve and come in if needed. But, there was no longer a need for regularly scheduled appointments. We celebrated!

I asked Steve some questions. One was, "After seeing all I've been through and all the other patients you've dealt with, what positive things stick out for you about our time together?" Steve, who was in his seventies at the time, replied with something like, "You are the hardest working patient I have ever had. Many people think spending an hour in therapy a week is going to cure them. You figured it out - that there is a lot of work to be done between appointments. The day you said to me, 'Tell me how to fix me. I don't want to feel like this anymore' – I still remember that."

Then I asked Steve, "What is your biggest regret about our time together?" He replied, "That I didn't meet you when you were thirteen years old."

What I Learned

Finding the right therapist was crucial to my healing. Steve was recommended by the staff at 5 West, but that doesn't always work out. Here's what I learned about finding good trauma therapists:

- *Look for someone who specializes in trauma*
- *Ask about their experience with PTSD specifically*
- *Trust your gut - if you don't feel safe after a few sessions, it's okay to find someone else*
- *Don't be afraid to interview potential therapists before committing*

Red flags I learned to watch for: therapists who rush you, don't respect boundaries, or make you feel judged. Good therapists, like Steve, let you set the pace. And reality wise, when Steve retired, it took me three tries to find a new therapist that was a good fit.

PHYSICAL PAIN/
BACK INJURY

Before I dive into my story, I want to describe for you what PTSD is like. Maybe you, the reader, know, but maybe you don't. It could be helpful to you to understand and be a support to someone in your life who is struggling. And even if you do, it may be comforting to know that you are not alone.

Now, let's talk about what it is like to have PTSD. For me, pain is a known trigger. In this context, physical pain, that is. So, what is pain? We all know it when we feel it. It's like your brain sending off alarm bells to alert you that something bad is happening.

In the medical field, you've probably been asked a question like, "On a scale of one to ten how much pain are you in? One being very little and ten being the worst pain you've ever had." Sounds very individual and subjective, right? Well it is!

We will get more into the details later, but when I started physical therapy, I likely said I reached a ten on the pain scale when my leg gave out and I fell down – it felt like a big electrical shock and I gave a verbal yelp from pain. Later, I passed out from an even greater pain; that became my new ten, and the leg giving out was my nine. Then one day, I was in so much pain, I was pleading for an ambulance. You guessed it, my new ten! Passing out from pain became a nine and my leg giving out was now my eight.

Pain levels are very personal and based on our own experiences. To this day, I have never surpassed that experience of pleading for an ambulance as my ten. Thankfully!

Some forms of pain are more visible. We can see a wound. We can see a broken leg. We can see a black eye. We know it's painful when we see these things on others.

But, what if there is nothing to see. What if it is your soul that has been torn to shreds by pure evil? What if it is your very soul that is causing the most intense pain you have ever felt. Not only can we not see your pain, we can't see the wounds to your soul either. It is hard to have empathy if we don't know and can't see your pain.

If I walked into a gym on crutches (and I have), people come right over and ask how I'm doing. They offer help. They tell me their experiences with similar issues.

Now, when I walked into a gym with PTSD, there are no crutches; no leg braces; no wounds to see; no pain to see. In fact, no one knows you have PTSD unless you tell them. It's invisible.

What people may see is someone who is many things; tired, distracted, kind, caring, friendly, disconnected, anxious, detached, or asthmatic etc. Yeah, I also happen to have asthma. It could be triggered in the gym by a workout. Sometimes, it was made worse by PTSD. But people only knew I had asthma. It was a good cover. I didn't have to explain. I was afraid to share that I had PTSD.

Why? Because in most cases, when you tell someone you have PTSD, they naturally are curious and want to know what from. Some people say, "Oh, were you in the military? Police? Fire?" No one I know has ever said the thing that happened to me. So, I did everything I could to never say, "I have PTSD." Asthma was the obvious thing to point to when I was having difficulty and it was true. It just wasn't the entirety of the situation.

I marvel to this day at how different a physical injury is from PTSD. People showed me they cared. They saw an injury; they understood it. They offered support and encouragement.

It was not like the darkness that goes with PTSD. But what about my soul that needs healing? They can't see that either. You can see and touch a knee injury. But with trauma and PTSD, people who don't know can't see it.

As I mentioned, pain is a known trigger for me. So, let's talk about what it's like to be triggered...

What I Learned

Not everyone is trauma-informed, including medical providers. It doesn't mean they're bad people - they just don't know how trauma affects patients.
How to interact with trauma survivors:

- *Don't ask someone the source of their trauma — let them lead the conversation*
- *Let them know you care without pushing for details*
- *Listen without trying to "fix" or give advice unless asked*

How to advocate for yourself:

- *Tell providers what does and doesn't work for you*
- *Be specific about your triggers and needs*
- *Remember that you know your body and mind better than anyone*

Most healthcare providers genuinely want to help and will adjust their approach when you explain what you need. Don't be afraid to speak up - they're in the business of helping people and want to know what works best for you.

PTSD
TRIGGERS

BOOM! TRIGGERED! Your body goes into overdrive, launching you into fight or flight mode. The adrenaline rush taxes your body, your organs, and your mind. The exhaustion after a full-on trigger is like getting hit by a fully loaded double stack thundering freight train.

You can't turn it off. You have to deal with it. Whether you're at the grocery store, the gym, at work or taking your kids to school. PTSD doesn't ask you when it should surface. It surfaces at any time, in any moment, at any location it wants. And somehow, you have to learn to be ready for that and okay that it happens. I can tell you – sometimes you feel like your going crazy. I've learned coping skills are key to managing these unpredictable PTSD symptoms.

Over time, I've learned strategies that work for me in those moments to ground myself. I've figured out how to hide my internal PTSD explosions from those around me. Not every time of course.

Sometimes, I just walk away and find someplace to be alone. But, if I can keep it internal, the people around me may think I'm distracted or deep in thought. Some may think I'm grumpy and disengaged. Most describe it as, "Matt isn't himself today."

In my view, if I can get there – to where those around me just view me as not being myself during a full-on triggering event – it is a win. And every win matters.

Let's be real though. I've had triggers, flash backs and night terrors where I end up curled up in a ball on the floor crying, hyperventilating, and reliving the worst moments of my life. It's no picnic. And I also know, that over time these major symptoms can and will become fewer and farther apart and less intense.

So, what are potential triggers? Triggers could be a simple thought, a scene in a movie, a sight, a sound, a smell, touch, a place, a person, or how a stranger walks, the color of their hair or their mannerisms. Anything, that your brain connects to the traumatic event(s). It is as individual as the person with PTSD and as individual as the trauma itself.

Maybe the event for you, if you have PTSD, took place outside in the fall season. You could be triggered by the color of the leaves falling from the trees. Sometimes the triggers are obvious. Sometimes they don't make any sense at all and you can't associate or understand why you're triggered. Being thrown into fight or flight mode, your brain and body react like your life is in danger and you have no idea the source of the danger or what the trigger was! Now that's a PTSD party! That's the icing on the proverbial PTSD cake!

When those moments happen, I feel like I'm nuts! Full on bat shit crazy. But, I'm not and neither are you. It's just how our brains got re-wired from trauma. Our brains have associated these things with the memories and emotions of what happened to us. Just like it is happening all over again in real time. You mind doesn't know the difference. The subconscious mind believes it is happening! BOOM! DANGER!

The hardest thing for me about triggers is after they're over. I had to learn to just accept that it happened and move on from it. I used to be stuck in fear after they happened. "I need to avoid the trigger at all costs!" The only way to avoid a trigger was not to leave the house. But, I'll ask you the you the same question Steve asked me–- "You can stay home and never be triggered again. But, what kind of life is that?"

What I Learned

Developing your trigger management plan:

- *Make a list of known triggers and rate them (1-10 for intensity)*
- *Identify your early warning signs (heart racing, sweating, feeling dizzy)*
- *Develop grounding techniques: 5 things you can see, 4 you can hear, 3 you can touch, 2 you can smell, 1 you can taste*
- *Practice breathing exercises when you're NOT triggered so they're automatic when you need them*
- *Have a safety plan: Who can you call? Where can you go? What helps you feel safe?*
- *Know that triggers can change over time - what bothers you now might not in a year*
- *Don't judge yourself for being triggered - it's your brain trying to protect you*

Remember: avoiding all triggers isn't living. The goal is learning to manage them so they don't control your life.

ANXIETY

Anxiety is a big part of PTSD. We tend to "what if?" And boy, can we create the worst possible outcomes! I had many conversations with Steve about how I managed anxiety. Well, really, how I didn't manage anxiety. When you don't manage anxiety, you get into catastrophizing! And man! I really excel at catastrophizing! I'm a pro!

As I got healthier, I would go to therapy with a story about something that triggered me, how poorly I handled it and an idea on what I would try to do next time. Steve would say I was really good at figuring these things out after the fact. That wasn't a compliment. It was a gentle jab for me to get out ahead of it.

Steve would say, "There you go again Matt! From A to Z in a millisecond. You do know that there are twenty-four other letters you could stop at before you get to Z, right?"

We talked about ways to try to apply the brakes when catastrophizing starts. Try to get the mind to stop and take a breath. It wasn't easy. I'm better at it for sure now though I still haven't perfected it. But, it does work! And, it may work for you too!

The one thing that works for me more than anything else is to step *through* the anxiety. Whatever it is. Anxiety is about the future.

If you're anxious about something-- get it over with. Once it is in the past, you can't be anxious anymore because it is behind you. Trust me on this one. It works.

For example, you have a doctor's appointment coming up that you're worried about? Try to move that appointment up. If you can't, get on the cancellation list! Once the appointment is over, there's nothing that can cause anxiety. You can't be anxious about the past.

Are you worried how a family member will react to news you need to share? Stop thinking about it and call them. Get it behind you. Once it is behind you, you can't be anxious.

It works! It's a miracle cure and no meds needed! Give it a go!

FLASH BACKS

I'm dreading this topic but it is important to understanding PTSD before I tell you my story–- Flash Backs. So, what is a flashback? There are many movies now that try to depict characters having flashbacks. Sometimes, I think they get it. Sometimes, it's off the mark. But, again, I'm sure flashbacks are as unique to the person having them as the trauma is that they survived. What I do know is that I wouldn't wish the flashbacks I've had on anyone.

Because of how PTSD brains store memories, when you have a flashback, you are reliving the trauma. Every sight, sound, smell, and feeling like the pain you had is happening once again in real time right then. POW! Welcome back to the absolute worst moment(s) of your existence!

I'm not talking like going from a 2D movie to 3D or even 4D. I'm talking about your brain believing you are back in the room where it happened. Back to face your attacker. Back to the front lines in the war. Back to the accident you survived while holding a loved one who didn't. Back to the horror.

Oh wait, there's more! This isn't meant to be figurative. You guessed it! Your body; heart, lungs, muscles, skin–- absolutely every part of your physical being–- is literally reacting like you're back in the horror. Breathing fast, heart pounding, sweating, stomach turning and your brain in full flight or fight mode.

During a flashback you may curl up in a ball and rock back and forth. You may sob uncontrollably. You may scream. You may pass out. You may fight back like you did in real life when "IT" happened. Whatever the "IT" is for you.

I've had friends, medical providers and family see me when I've had a flashback. It isn't pretty. When I've settled down, and after the flashback is over, I always ask the same thing, "Did I keep you safe?"

I don't ask what happened. I was there. I lived it. I just remembered and relived the horror again. I don't want to know what it looks like to see me having a flashback. I've got enough on my plate to try to recover from the memories I just relived.

I am so thankful for all those that were at my side during those moments. Those people; my family, friends, medical providers and others who cared. They held my hand. They hugged me. They told me I was safe.

While the flashback ran its course, I knew I wasn't alone. On some level I could feel their touch. I could hear their reassurance that I was safe. I also tried to listen to their voice. Their reassuring voices were like a light to walk to–- to get out. It helped as I tried to pull myself out of the noise in my head, the horror in my head.

These very human gestures from people who care about me, shorten the flashbacks and the time I relived the trauma in these moments. I am forever grateful for all the people who have walked my journey with me.

One time, I was volunteering at an event to provide Christmas gifts to those in need. There was a guy there who stood out. At first he seemed to be looking for things for his young child. Then I noticed, he started looking around like he was lost. Then he became more frenetic about it. I could see he was having a moment of panic. I've seen that before. I've lived that before. I walked over to him, told him my name and asked if I could help him find a place to sit down.

He was stuttering, struggling to breathe. When we sat down, I reassured him that he was safe and that I was there to help. I could see the tears well up in his eyes. He was frightened. I told him that it appeared to me that he might be having a panic attack, I'm familiar with them and I asked his permission to put my hand on his shoulder to ground him. He nodded in agreement.

I put my hand on his shoulder and continued to calmly tell him he was safe. That I was there with him and I wasn't going to leave him. He was not alone. I suggested that we breathe together. In deeply, hold and then out slowly. I knew he could hear me as he was trying to breathe with me. His eyes continued to dart around the room like he was looking for danger.

I asked him to try to focus on me. On my eyes. He tried to do that. But, he was frightened. I could see he felt like he needed to see where everyone in the room was. I continued to calmly talk to him and continued to keep my hand on him to reassure him he was not alone. Touch can be a grounding technique for some.

After about ten to fifteen minutes his breathing slowed and he began to relax. Once he settled down, was back in the present and able to communicate–- he told me he gets triggered by chaotic places–- shopping malls, lots of people etc. He was scared to walk through the crowd but still wanted to get presents for his child.

I asked what he was looking for and we got it for him. I then offered to walk him out and offered to take his hand while we did that. He calmed even more. When he was ready, we got up, I carried the gifts in one hand and held his hand with the other. We walked through the crowd and out the door. Once he was outside he calmed considerably more. He gave me a hug and wished me a merry Christmas and headed home.

While I don't know what his trauma was–- I do know he needed someone to help him through it. I was glad I was there. I felt like my past trauma had just served a purpose. It felt good to help someone else instead of being helped. It was encouraging to use my knowledge of how to manage my own triggers to help him through his. Especially during the holidays.

What I Learned

How to help someone having a panic attack or flashback:

- *Stay calm and speak in low, reassuring tones*
- *Ask permission before touching - never grab or restrain someone*
- *Help them focus on the present: "You're safe," "I'm here with you," "This is 2025, not the past"*
- *Encourage slow, deep breathing*
- *Don't take their reactions personally - they're not really "seeing" you in that moment*
- *Give them space and time to recover - Don't ask for details about what they experienced - that's for later, with their therapist*

What NOT to do: Don't tell them to "calm down" or "get over it." Don't leave them alone unless they specifically ask you to.

PTSD NIGHT TERRORS

Now I just mentioned what can happen during the day. The worst time for me is at night. That's when the real fun begins! Sure, I have strategies I've used before bed. Things like keeping a routine; going to bed around the same time; brushing my teeth; maintaining a certain temperature in the bedroom; bed made; running some white noise (my favorite is a fan); and, reading until I'm ready to fall asleep.

So what is it like when that doesn't work? Nighttime can be brutal. One thing that happens is that at night external noise and distractions decrease significantly. When external distractions go away, our PTSD mind is free to wake up and fill the silence with whatever makes us uncomfortable. The PTSD monster awakens! Trying not to feed that monster is the strategy.

So, let's say, we finally get to sleep. At that point, we are at our PTSD brain's mercy. We can't control what we dream. We can't control where our brains lead us. Nor can we control what the subconscious mind decides it needs to process.

I've tried to explain sleeping with PTSD this way to friends and family: Everyone dreams. Sometimes we remember, sometimes we don't. Sometimes we all have nightmares. This could be the old favorite humorous one where you're speaking to a crowd and realize you're naked.

Or there is the brutal nightmare. In this type, a family member may be killed in front of you and you bolt upright. You're soaked in sweat! Your heart is pounding! You reach for the phone thinking you should check in on them. You're not quite sure you can trust that it was just a nightmare. It was too real.

The worst of the worst for me is what I refer to as the PTSD night terror. This is my term for it. And it is vastly worse than a brutal nightmare. Here you are not only having the worst of the worst most brutal nightmare in your head, but you are also physically participating in it in real life.

This could mean thrashing in bed like you're having a seizure or trying to physically fight off the horror in your brain. Maybe like me, you've gotten out of bed and run down the hall to save your children from the evil your brain concocted. I've even found myself outside of my house when I've awakened from a night terror.

Night terrors are dangerous. I do everything I can to avoid them. They scare me a great deal. Bad things can happen when you're physically moving around during a PTSD night terror.

When I was talking to Steve about them, he suggested I try to find something during the night terror that doesn't make sense while they are happening. At first I thought it was ridiculous. How can I do that if I'm asleep? But, the mere fact that I'm moving around during one means I'm sort of awake too. That finally clicked with me.

On two occasions I recall it worked. One time in my night terror, I was inside a room. I looked up for a way to escape. And, when I looked up I saw stars. I was actually outside in real life. That snapped me out of it.

Another time, I was running to get into my house. But the house I was running toward was painted blue. My house is tan. That also got me out of the night terror. Steve's suggestion was working!

I don't claim that this type of stuff will work for everyone. Dealing with PTSD symptoms and coping skills is very individual. I tried many things before I figured out what worked for me. And sometimes, those things that worked for me–- well, sometimes even those things don't work. The only thing I find consistent about PTSD is that it can be inconsistent.

And when something doesn't work, you need to be open to trying some-thing new. Trying something new can be scary. I get it. Being scared is a form of anxiety. How do you handle anxiety? You step through it. Be open to finding what works for you. You can get there. I have and when you succeed, it is empowering, rewarding and worth celebrating!

What I Learned

Safety planning for night terrors:

- *Remove or secure anything dangerous from your bedroom*
- *Consider sleeping on the ground floor to avoid stairs*
- *Tell people you live with what to expect and how to help*
- *Keep your bedroom simple and familiar so you can orient yourself*
- *Some people benefit from motion-sensor lights that turn on automatically*
- *Consider wearing a medical alert bracelet if you sleepwalk during terrors*

If you live with someone who has night terrors: Don't try to wake them forcefully. Speak calmly, turn on lights, and try to guide them back to safety. It's scary to watch, but they usually don't remember it.

Chapter 4

THE HEALING TEAM

PAUL, PHYSICAL THERAPIST #2

While working with Steve, I was still walking around with a cane due to my back and leg issues. I went to Rundlett Middle School for one of my kids' functions and I ran into a parent, Paul, of another child I knew. I had seen him at birthday parties and stuff and at this point, I didn't know much about him.

Paul walked up to me and asked me about the cane I was using to walk with and what type of care I was getting for my injuries. I told him that I had been to a lot of physical therapy, made good progress but had some setbacks. I was taking a break because nothing seemed to work. He told me that he was a physical therapist and suggested I reach out to him and he'd see what he could do for me.

Over time I did reach out to him, but, I also had information I didn't have with my first PT, Mark. I had by now been diagnosed with PTSD and one of the most significant triggers I was aware of is being touched. Yup! How can you possibly go to physical therapy and not be touched! My anxiety about the appointment was through the roof.

Now, think back to what I shared about my first PT. Remember how I described having anxiety, panic attacks, hyperventilating, and passing out? Those are all possible PTSD responses to being triggered. But, back then I didn't know I had PTSD. I thought those symptoms were brought on by pain. And guess what? They were. They could have been brought on from physical pain or brain pain. I had plenty of both.

At some point I shared with him that I had PTSD and touch could be a trigger. I didn't want him to put anything about PTSD in my medical record. I wasn't ready to share that but he needed to know. We set things up for longer appointments and always in a private exam room. I felt safer with four walls around me. There was less my mind and my hypervigilance would have to process and keep track of. It allowed me to be more present and grounded.

At our appointments we would talk first, agree to how the appointment was going to go and then Paul would ask permission to touch me and wait for my reply. We built trust this way.

One day, something happened, and I went into a full-on panic attack. I was lying on the exam table shaking, crying and hyperventilating. Paul did the most natural and human thing he could. He leaned over, hugged me tight and told me I was safe. I remember feeling safe. Like a child who skinned their knee and ran to mom or dad for comfort and safety in their embrace.

Because of my needs PTSD-wise, the physical therapy appointments became more frequent and we got less done because of the need to talk before and after each session to help me manage the PTSD noise in my head. At some point management at the facility told Paul that he had to let me go as they felt I wasn't making fast enough physical progress and they were concerned about their numbers. You know - the numbers insurance companies care about. Money comes before patients type stuff. Yeah, folks, it's real.

After hearing this from his management, Paul called my doctor (PCP), and told my doctor what was up and suggested that Paul could do more for me as my friend than he could as my PT due to all the hospital regulations that were getting in the way. His intentions were only good and in my best interest.

When I was told physical therapy with Paul was coming to an end, I completely freaked out. Trust was broken! I was lied to! It was a significant set-back in my healing. A setback for PTSD. A setback for trust.

I trusted someone and they quit on me. I quickly learned that trust violations, or should I say perceived violations of trust in this case, were another huge trigger for my PTSD.

Now in Paul's role as my friend, he came to my house that night, as he was concerned about how I was handling the news. And Steve happened to call me while he was there.

I was short circuiting. Safety was gone! Trust was shattered! Hope was lost! Train completely off the rails! I would never heal! Oh yeah, I was catastrophizing big time! Can you tell?!?

During this time, it was brutal on me as a human being. My mind exploded. I can look back at it now as a blip in my journey. Back then it was the worst thing that could have happened to me and it felt like it went on forever. Hope was diminished, if not destroyed, that I could heal.

Paul did keep his word in the end. He would swing by my house before or after work and we'd continue to work on physical therapy stuff and we rebuilt the trust we had. The PTSD symptoms were intense for me. It was a lot for him too. But, we found our way through it all.

At one point, while Paul was helping me with physical therapy stuff, Steve told me I needed to tell my story to heal. Whatever part I felt I could share, with anyone. Steve said it didn't have to be him, but I needed to share something with someone. I needed to crack THE BOX open just a little.

I called Paul and told him my assignment from Steve. He came over as soon as he could and we sat in my living room one night and I shared. Just a little bit. THE BOX was opened slightly for the very first time.

I was worried what Paul was going to think. How would he react? After I finished telling him and crying, I asked him what he was thinking. Paul replied, "That was the hardest thing I've ever heard. I could feel your pain in what you went through."

Back then, what I shared was a small piece of the story. A piece I was healthy enough to get out. But, I shared it. I said it out loud and Paul heard me. He didn't reject me and by his own words, he felt my pain as he heard what I chose to share of my story. I remember thinking, maybe I'm not alone in this after all. Maybe I can heal. Maybe I won't be rejected when people hear it.

Paul remains one of the most important people on my journey. I think of him often. The fact that Paul adapted for my PTSD needs – longer appointments, private rooms, asking permission before touching – showed me what trauma-informed care really looks like.

What I Learned

What I learned about finding trauma-informed healthcare providers:

- *Look for providers who ask about your comfort level and check in regularly*
- *Good providers will modify their approach when you explain your triggers*
- *They should be willing to take extra time and have longer appointments if needed*
- *Ask upfront if they have experience working with trauma patients*
- *Don't settle for providers who dismiss your concerns or make you feel like you're "difficult"*

Paul's willingness to use private rooms and ask permission before touching me showed he understood trauma responses, even before I fully explained my PTSD.

ADAM, DOCTOR OF OSTEOPATHIC MEDICINE

Part 1

During my official physical therapy time with Paul, it became clear that my back issues continued to dominate my physical pain, and the care I needed was complicated by PTSD symptoms.

So, after a lot of prodding by my PCP, Sean, (now my friend and an all-round awesome human) and other medical providers, I agreed to see a doctor of osteopathic medicine. His name is Adam. He is a physiatrist (pain specialist).

Adam worked for the same company based in Bedford where a different doctor had quit on me. Even though Adam was in Concord, I was very hesitant to step foot in his office because of my experience in Bedford. Trust with his employer had been broken, so to speak.

During my first visit with Adam, there was a book in the waiting room that shouldn't have been there. That book was a trigger. I was angry that it was there. Trust was already breaking with Adam and I hadn't even met him yet. Oh, I'm sure your wondering what the book is, right? We will get to that later.

I walked into the exam room. At one end was a large desk which Adam sat behind with his computer and then on my side was an exam table for me. It was set up like an office with an exam table in it. Very clinical and cold.

I got triggered and told Adam that I wasn't comfortable. My anxiety yelled at me, "This was a power move on his part to be behind a large desk and leave me out in the open. Like a deer in the field waiting to be shot." Ah ha! Another trigger - power dynamics. I need to feel equal with my doctors. Not less than.

Learning one's triggers is a key to minimizing their impacts on your health. Now we knew some triggers; Trust; Touch; and Power Dynamics.

Adam without hesitation, got up and walked over to me and sat down on his wheeled stool. He wanted me to feel comfortable. He started asking me some questions and then listened like no back doctor I'd ever had before him. I mean he listened. Really listened!

He didn't look at his watch. He was genuinely interested in my story like a detective looking for clues to find a solution to my pain. And then I suddenly burst into tears and said, "I need you to help me heal my soul!"

I'm not sure what went through Adam's head in that moment. But, I imagine that that was the first and only time he's heard that request from a patient! I mean after all how do you heal one's soul?

That said, Adam is a one of a kind person and doctor. His view on pain is that the patient needs to be treated as a human being first and foremost. This was new to me. I wasn't just a diagnosis. I recall him saying once, "You don't treat the X-ray. You treat the person."

We began working together on finding ways to heal. He convinced me to go back to physical therapy with someone he had worked closely with in the past. He felt this PT would communicate well with him and he would have close insight into how things were progressing.

Adam is one of the few physicians that actually reads the PT's notes. Other doctors may have a nurse or admin take a look and alert them if something is off. Not Adam. This man truly cares for each and every person that steps into his office.

So, I agreed to Adam's plan and agreed to work with this new PT, Jason. I also checked in with Paul to make sure Jason was on the up and up. I asked if I could trust Jason. Paul gave him a great reference and reassured me that it was going to be okay.

This was a lot for me. I was returning to the place that just quit on me, with a new PT to try again. This time would be different. This time, Adam was directly involved.

JASON, PHYSICAL THERAPIST #3

I met the new PT, Jason, at the same facility where I used to see Paul. I was very hesitant to go back there. I still blamed the management there for cutting me off before we had finished last time. But, this time I was assured by Adam that he and Jason would work together closely on my case and no one would end my care without me being part of the process.

By the time I met Jason, I had learned a lot about PTSD. I understood which things could be triggers and I was able to articulate those to him.

The more I could share the better it was for both of us. We'd both know what triggers to avoid, so we could focus more of our time together on physical therapy. I chalked that up to growth from what I learned with Paul – proof that I was starting to get some control back over the chaos that is PTSD.

Jason and I set up a routine and used a private treatment room like I had before. We created routines which we used at each appointment - talk first and touch second, and talk again. That process helped diminish the possibilities of triggers.

Oh, don't get me wrong, I still got triggered when I was with Jason. I remember one time I was triggered by a tiny red light. You know, those red lights on a fire alarm that let you know it has power.

He could see what I was looking at while I was panicking and figured this trigger out on his own. At the next appointment, I went into the room and the light had been covered with black electrical tape.

I knew Jason did that for me. He never said a word about it. He just cared about me and saw a simple solution to help me be healthy while I was with him.

Sometimes, after treatment, I would just stay in the room until I settled down while he went on to his next patient. When I was ready and felt composed, I would leave on my own.

We were making good progress – but once again, it wasn't fast enough for management. They ended treatment on me again, over everyone else's objection.

This time, my PTSD went so out of whack, I hopped on a catastrophizing train and left the station. Fully suicidal. I don't remember all the details. My head wasn't clear. Yup! That's an understatement.

I'm aware that Sean, and the management team exchanged words about my situation. Sean felt that the Hippocratic oath - "Do no harm" – had been totally disregarded by management.

Sean's nurse, gave me a call while I was suicidal. She was awesome. She worked with me to help settle things down to get me to come back to the present. I'm not sure if she knew that I was suicidal or not. That's the thing about PTSD. You don't think clearly in the moment; sometime it's hard to put words together and what you think and what you share may not be the same. It's chaos. But, she could tell I needed help.

At the end of it, everyone agreed that I would return to physical therapy and do two more weeks with Jason to create a healthy off-ramp to reduce the harm that management had caused once again.

After we finished our very last appointment together, I stayed in the exam room and Jason went on to his next patient. I climbed up on the exam table and took the electrical tape off the little red light and placed it on the keyboard of the computer. It was my way of saying, "Look at how far we've come. Thank you and I noticed."

Jason and I remain friends to this day. I respect and trust him a great deal. To this day, even when lots of time passes without touching base, we know we have each other's back.

ADAM, DOCTOR OF OSTEOPATHIC MEDICINE

Part 2

After the management debacle at the physical therapy clinic, Adam stepped in and took over my full care, including physical therapy duties. The setback I had PTSD-wise was brutal on me. Trust with everyone was destroyed. It was like starting over again.

I needed patterns. I needed consistency. I needed trust. I needed safety. I needed to know I wasn't going to be abandoned or lied to again. I would not be going back to that physical therapy clinic ever again. NEVER! Not even if hell froze over.

Management there almost cost me my life - twice. But the PTs were awesome. They knew that everyone should be treated like a person, encompassing all that they are dealing with, not just an injury, or worse just numbers on a piece of paper.

Adam and I talked a lot before I would agree to any next steps. He was doing what he could to rebuild trust with me. After all, it was Adam who sent me to that physical therapy clinic. And with my inability to trust, even though it was management at that physical therapy clinic that screwed things up, I still associated that illogically with Adam too.

In the end, we agreed that I would be Adam's last patient of the day every Tuesday, until we both agreed to a different schedule. He assured me that as the Doctor he could set the appointments for himself. No one was going to interfere between him and I, like management had at the physical therapy clinic.

This new approach with Adam began to build the trust I needed to heal my back pain and, in turn, to start peeling back the onion to begin to heal my soul.

(Note: Since writing this book, management at the physical therapy clinic has changed. They have improved their processes, taking mental health and the whole human into account. I believe they are learning. After all, they are humans too and being human means being imperfect. I'm thankful for their continued growth and focus on trauma-informed care.)

PHYSICAL THERAPY

I can't say enough about all of the physical therapists (PTs) I've seen. To this day, I'm friends with nearly all of them. It's hard not to become friends with someone who willingly steps in the trenches with you and who, no matter how hard things got, never gave up on you. A friendship formed in the trenches is solid, unwavering, and reliable. I'm so fortunate to have had many PTs who were that for me.

Things didn't always go well in physical therapy. I learned a lot about physical therapy, insurance companies, hospital bureaucracy and most importantly, pain. Yeah, there's that word again - pain. You know the word - the one that can lead to suicidal thoughts.

Interestingly, throughout my time with suicidal ideations, I don't recall a single time that I thought, "I want to die." For me, though it could be different for you, it was always about pain. "I can't take the pain any longer. I need to end this pain."

The pain meds didn't always help, so I felt there was no way out. I've learned that's not the case and there are always options.

Now the hard part is to realize that there are always options when your mind is telling you have only one choice, a permanent choice. This is what coping skills are for. This is what friends are for. This is what 988 is for.

I like to keep busy, if the noise is filling my head with unwanted thoughts, in order to quiet it down. If that doesn't work, I call my friends or take appropriate meds to assist. Or, if you can, call 988. Note that 988 became available the year I wrote this book. I didn't have access to that number during my recovery.

We will get into suicidal thoughts further. But, for now, please know there are always options. Stay connected with friends, family or just be around people if the thoughts become overwhelming. Being alone, at least for me, fueled the ideations.

And if you're having suicidal thoughts right now - remember this - Suicide is a permanent solution to a temporary problem. Call 988 right now and let them know what's going on. They're there to help!

And, I need you to keep reading! So, hang with me - tell the thoughts to screw off and get the hell out of your head. You are in the middle of reading a book! And who knows, this book might just help you and maybe give you hope for your situation.

So, against such a negative message in my head, what did physical therapy do for me? It prepared me for the hardest part of my healing journey – finally confronting what I had locked away for decades.

Chapter 5

OPENING THE BOX

THE BOX

Okay. Here we are. Staring at THE BOX. It deserves all caps. Everyone's box is different. Everyone's trauma is as unique as the people who are traumatized.

What I'm about to share is my BOX. Well, I'm not likely going to share *everything* in THE BOX. But I will share enough so you have context.

My legs are bouncing. I'm sweating. My heart is racing. I'm triggered just trying to figure out what to share. I'm triggered because I'm remembering the things that are in THE BOX. I'm actively choosing to look in THE BOX to write this book.

This box has been in the deepest darkest corner of my mind for decades. I only opened this box fifteen years or so ago. To know that I'm essentially sharing its contents with the world (well at least strangers like you who choose to read this) is scary.

Let's start with who doesn't know what's in this BOX. My parents. My mom died when I was twenty-seven. I hadn't opened THE BOX back then. My dad died when I was forty-nine. I had every opportunity to share with my dad. But I chose not to. He didn't know about my PTSD nor did he know the source. And my aunt, who was like a second mother to me. I didn't want her to know. She died a couple of years ago.

I thought many times about talking more publicly about what happened to me. But I decided to wait until my parents and my aunt passed. I just didn't want them to feel like they made any mistakes. They didn't. Maybe,

I was saving myself from having to share. I feel more like I was doing them a favor. I didn't want them to know what happened to me - not for my sake, but for theirs.

Now, I'm thinking about my siblings. Some who know and some don't. Some who know the source. Some don't. Now, they will, if they choose to read this.

To those that know me, I'm still the same person you've always known. In fact, my trauma helped make me who I am today. And as surprising as this may sound - I wouldn't change a thing. I like who I am. I like that I survived. It made me stronger. It made me more empathetic.

Let's start with the easy part...no it's not really easy...but it is easier than the next part...let's talk about where I grew up - Royal Gardens. Sounds like a nice place, right?

ROYAL GARDENS

Royal Gardens, located on the heights in Concord, NH, is a 260-unit low-income housing complex built in the 1970's.

Calling something Royal and planting the imagery of Gardens was probably good marketing back in the day. It was anything other than the image the name brings to mind. It was the projects. It was high crime. It was drug infested. It was violent. It was my childhood home.

Most of my life-long friends grew up here. We marvel now that we survived. We focus on how far we've come into adulthood. We made it out. We were the lucky ones. And yes, we were all damaged by it.

In the most formative years of our lives we had to figure out how to keep ourselves safe. I lived there from three to fifteen years old.

We didn't know any better; it was the way it was. We had nothing to compare it to. But now, looking back, it's a rough story.

Each of my friends has their own take on how they grew up there. Here I'm going to focus on my own experiences. But, I can tell you, if they wrote a book - I'd buy it.

This is how my most formative years of my life were formed. How I learned to be strong. Honestly, I didn't have a choice. To be a "Heights Boy" as we refer to ourselves, you had to be tough. You had to have thick skin or you'd be eaten alive. But, that environment doesn't come without a cost.

I remember being threatened in sixth grade for an eternity by a bully named Wayne. He was always threatening me, to the point that I was afraid to get off the school bus if he was there.

One day, my brother, Brad, who is three years older than me, was going to meet me at the bus stop to protect me from Wayne. My brother was a few minutes late or the bus was early - who knows…

I got off the bus, and Wayne punched me in the mouth and beat the snot out of me. He split my lip open, blood was everywhere, I was crying while running home. The blood was coming through my hand as I covered my mouth. My face, my shirt were covered in blood.

When my brother got there, he beat the crap out of Wayne. Slammed his head into a car windshield, I was told. Today, Wayne is a resident of the NH State Prison for men. He is serving nearly thirty years for aggregated felonious sexual assault. I share just to give you an idea what kind of kids lived in the projects.

Violence was as normal as the sun coming up in the east. Even as friends we fought with each other. We would taunt each other to the point that a fight would break out. That was normal and okay. Or at least we thought it was normal. We didn't know any better. But, if someone who wasn't our friend messed with any one of us, we were steadfast and united.

Each apartment had a front door leading outside. These apartments were set up like town houses. Each door had a mail slot. The mailman would open the slot and push the mail through. The mail landed on the living room floor. You could look through those mail slots. In fact, some people did - peeping Tom's. Others would use the opening to drop flaming things in to set apartments on fire.

Going to the city pool in the summer was a test of your ability to outrun or outthink the other gangs. I call them gangs. But, they were just another large family or another group of kids who weren't our friends. And if they weren't our friends, they were potential adversaries. Danger.

This is how we thought. How I thought. You want to go to the pool? You go in a group. You want to leave the pool - you do it together. The more people we had together the safer we were.

I was never much of a fighter as kid. Oh sure, I fought. Sometimes, I didn't have a choice. And I also knew people, my friends, who were better at fighting than I was. It was safer to be with them.

Once I fought a kid, who was bigger than I was, across the street from my apartment. But, this kid didn't want to fight me. He knew he could've beat the crap out of me.

He just put his hand on my head while I was swinging wildly at him. Then he'd just push me to the ground and laugh. I'd get back up and go after him again. He laughed more and shoved me to the ground again. But, he never punched me. He was in control.

Another time, a kid wouldn't leave the sand pit, I was throwing rocks near him to get him to move. He didn't and I inadvertently hit him in the head with a rock. He bled a lot. I've always felt bad about that.

Long before the "Just say no" campaign, Royal Gardens was a drug haven. And with drugs comes violence. I remember a time that something was going on with my brother. Someone came to the apartment to tell us my brother was in danger. I heard my parents talking about drugs. My father took off to get him. To this day, I don't know what happened.

Survival of the fittest. That's what it was like. You either had to be at the top of the food chain, which I wasn't, or you had to be smart to stay out of danger. Every time you left your apartment, you stepped into potential danger. Fight or flight.

The adults in Royal Gardens could be just as dangerous as the kids. Actually more dangerous. I had one guy convince me to go into his apartment to see his comic book collection. There were comics, and there was porn. He had a whole room filled with metal book shelving and porn everywhere. Fight or flight.

Another guy who worked at a produce stand allowed us kids to go in and set the fruit and vegetables out. It was fun. Something we didn't get to do. We got to see how a store really works! That led to friendship and an invitation to a lake house. Holy crap! We knew someone with a lake house!

A buddy of mine who was a couple years older and I went to the lake house. It turned out that the invitation was just a way for the guy to see us put on our swim trunks. Yea, one room cottage. No privacy. Creep.

Unfortunately, that friend of mine ended up in jail himself. Unmarried with many kids and to this day I hear he's still struggling with alcoholism. I hope he gets his chance at redemption one day.

Walking to Dame School, our local grade school, was no picnic either. We'd take short cuts through the woods. One time we found what we thought was a dead body in a sleeping bag. No tent. Just a sleeping bag in the bushes.

We kicked it to see if they were dead. We freaked out when the person in the sleeping bag moved and we ran as fast as we could. Just a normal morning in the projects on our way to 1st and 2nd grade class.

My friends in Royal Gardens all faced their own struggles. Alcoholic parent(s), a family member who was a rapist, physical beatings from their parent(s) and the list could go on and on. Fear was everywhere. But, we learned to cover up that fear with being tough. Or, at least, *acting* tough.

I mentioned earlier we had to have thick skin. Even from our closest friends. We were ruthless to each other. If you were different in any way, you better toughen up because your closest friend was going to point it out and torment you in front of everyone. The more people around, the more likely the topic would be brought up.

In the 1980s and living in the projects, when you did something someone thought was stupid - you were "gay" or you liked something someone else didn't like - you'd hear, "That's so gay." Did something really stupid - "You're such a faggot." Political correctness didn't exist. Tearing each other down was the norm.

Whatever we were dealing with in our own lives as a kid, we took it out on our friends. That's how we dealt with things. All the tension inside of us would turn into an outburst towards each other or the "lesser" kids.

You know the ones - the kids who couldn't defend themselves. They were low on the food chain. As a group we were relentless. That's just the way things were.

Maybe you are wondering where our parents were? There was no such thing as helicopter parenting when I grew up. We did what we wanted when we wanted. We had more freedom as kids than you'd believe.

I remember recently saying to a buddy who grew up with me, "Man, we had a lot of freedom growing up." He replied, "I wouldn't call it freedom. We were unsupervised. There's a big difference."

Yeah, that weighs heavy on me. It was probably the biggest reason I was so involved in my kids' lives. Keep them safe. Be there for them. Give them the things I didn't have.

There's no question my parents loved me and my brother. The four of us lived in Building 1, Apartment 10. It was an end unit in our building. My longest living friend on the planet lived right next door in Apartment 9. He knows the following truths better than anyone other than my brother and I.

We lived in low-income housing for a reason. We didn't have much. I recall vividly an argument between my mother and father about whether they should buy a gallon of milk OR a loaf of bread. At that moment they couldn't afford both.

I recall my mother going down to get us food from the food bank. Things like a block of cheese. I don't remember why I remember the cheese. Probably because it was wrapped in plain white paper with no indication what it was – kind of mysterious.

But for some reason, my parents always found a way to have a good Christmas for my brother and I. We always had stockings, and there were always presents under the tree. Maybe they were trying to make up for the year that had just happened to us.

My dad, a good and complicated man, did everything he could to provide for us. At times, he was working three jobs. He was absent a lot.

Whenever he was home, he'd be in bed. He'd watch TV in bed and fall in and out of sleep. As a kid, I never saw him drink alcohol. Not once. He didn't have to; my mother was drinking more than enough for both of them. Her drink of choice - vodka.

My mom - I love my mom. She was saddled with a horrible disease - Alcoholism. She struggled to overcome it. And she finally did. But, by the time she did, her life had been shortened. She died at fifty-eight.

She redeemed herself in every way once she stopped drinking. She told me once, "I'm gonna spend the rest of my life, making up for the first twelve years of yours." I never forgot that. Never will.

And she did make up for it in every way. If there ever was someone who redeemed themselves in every way, it was my mom.

She was also the most religious person I knew - even to this day. A devout Catholic. No matter what was thrown at her, how many times she was knocked down, how many new diseases she faced - God was in her life. She carried a rosary with her at all times.

She was a talented musician. She played guitar and sang. Before Johnny Cash was famous, she was one of his backup singers at the Lone Star Ranch in Manchester when he'd come through.

She and her sisters sang live on WKXL as the "Stafford Sisters" and she was in a band called the Country Rockers. She wrote several religious songs.

Her religious beliefs grew stronger when life was unkind to her. She knew she was dying. They gave her ten years to live after a liver bypass operation and she lived thirteen years.

She was full of mischief. Always cagey, and looking for things to laugh about. She was always up to something funny to get us laughing.

In fact, one Christmas Day, she was in the hospital. We decided to celebrate Christmas with her in her hospital room. She got us laughing so hard, that one of the nurses came in to tell us to quiet down because, "There are sick people in other rooms."

We thought that was ironic and funny, because my mother had recently come out of another coma. We laughed more, but this time tried to be hushed about it.

When she drank, though, she wasn't that kind and caring mom I got to see before she died. She was a brutal vicious drunk. The alcoholic woman was not my mom. She became something different.

I don't blame my mom for anything that happened when she was drunk. Alcoholism is a disease. It destroys the drinker and it damages those who have to live with them.

When I'd come home from school, I'd never know what to expect when I opened the door. She might be passed out on the floor. She might throw a glass plate my way. She might scream this primal noise that was ear-piercing and more scary than you could possibly imagine. I knew, when I went home, I might not be safe. But, when you're young, where else do you go?

I don't remember ever having a birthday celebration until my mom was sober. At sixteen, that was the first one I remember having. To this day I try to remember everyone's birthday. I don't want people to be forgotten.

It's my way of making up for the birthdays I didn't have as a kid. It makes me feel good to reach out on someone's birthday even if it's just a text. They weren't forgotten. And I get to remember them and sometimes they give me an update about where they are in life.

For me, as a kid, I felt invisible. I stayed out of the house as much as possible. And when I was home, I was always tip-toeing around. Trying not to set someone off. Trying to not trigger someone's anger. My dad had a temper too. He'd yell a lot.

I remember hiding in a closet more than once. I even used a cardboard box as a fort in the closet to feel safer. I'd run into the closet and then into the box when things got real bad. There's those words again, "THE BOX."

Oh, and the record player. Always a sign of danger. We had one of those LP record players where when the needle reached the end of vinyl album it just stayed there as the record spun. And as the album kept spinning you'd hear it "scratch, scratch, scratch" as the record went around and round.

That sound haunts me. That means my mother was too drunk to lift the needle off the record - she was either passed out or violence was about to ensue. If I lifted the needle off the record she might come out of her stupor and scream at me for stopping the music.

Not only were things thrown at us, there were many physical fights including between my mother and father. Usually my mother attacked him when the vodka got too much for her. He would grab her wrists so she couldn't strike him. I would hide under the kitchen table and cover my ears.

I remember a fight between my brother and father. They were shoving each other into the walls. I was trying to stop it and my mother got between them, glass smashed on the floor and my mother cut her foot wide open. Blood everywhere.

Another time my mother shoved a bowl of ice cream in my face because I annoyed her. My crime, I had interrupted her drinking by asking her to stir the ice cream. I didn't like the lumps, I told her. But, what I really wanted was my mother's attention.

I remember overhearing my mom and aunt talking about how the Sisters of the Carmelite Monastery in Concord saved my mother's life. My mother would go there when she was drunk. They would take her in and keep her safe until she was sober.

I remember when my mom drank to a point that she became that other person, the drunk one, a neighbor would come over. I recall my father coming home and throwing the neighbor down the stairs and out the front door. I can only imagine why.

My brother, who was three years older than me, was dealing with things differently than I was. He got into drinking and stuff. I say stuff because he thought he was protecting me from the stuff. He wouldn't let me hang out with him. But, I knew the stuff was going on.

I thought he didn't want to be around me as I was not cool or because I was three years younger. What I didn't know until later in life is that he thought he was protecting me from alcohol and the stuff. We've talked a lot about that in adulthood. I get it now. He was trying to keep me safe the best way he knew how.

He and I are truly the only two who know what our childhoods were like. We remain very close to this day. I love my brother with all my heart and soul.

When I was twelve, I was woken up by my dad in the middle of the night. He told me to run down and get in the car. My dad and my brother carried my mother to the car and put her in the back seat with my brother. My dad jumped in the front seat.

I looked back and my mother was vomiting blood all over my brother. She was at death's door. The drinking had finally caught up with her.

This is the moment in my life that I always think about when someone asks me why I've never drank alcohol or done drugs. This is one of the many moments that haunts me – so much blood.

I can't imagine what was going through my brother's head as he held our mother in the back seat and she spewed blood all over him. We've talked about it some. We both remember it clearly and uncomfortably. Those images and that moment scarred us for life.

The good news here is that that was the last time my mother ever drank. She quit cold turkey. She didn't have a choice. It was vodka or her life. She chose to fight for her life. She became even more faithful to God.

She had emergency surgery. A portacaval shunt operation. A bypass of the liver. After that surgery, her blood had to circulate twice before it was cleaned of toxins by the liver. That became the start of terrible health issues.

After that operation, she became diabetic, had high ammonia levels, had many mini strokes, was in at least three comas that I recall, was declared clinically dead, only to find her way back to life, then had several more mini strokes, significantly lost her ability to hear, had to relearn how to speak, and later she was wheelchair-bound.

In the end she was diagnosed with pulmonary hypertension - high blood pressure of the lungs. Over the course of six months or so, her lungs filled with fluid until she drowned and died.

My dad and I tagged teamed taking care of my mom since my brother lived out of state. One day, after a distressing call from my dad, I stopped by to check on her after a call from my dad and found her dead body lying on the couch clutching the top end of the blanket she was laying under. The image haunts me to this day.

My mom was a great woman of extraordinary faith (even at the worst of times) who stumbled into alcoholism, found her way out of it, and into redemption. She is the reason that I believe everyone deserves a second chance. She earned it. I love my mom.

On the back of her headstone it reads, "Please don't shed a tear as you walk by. For as you are now, so once was I. For as I am now, you too will become. So enjoy life, laugh, and have some fun."

I love you Mom!

My dad was a strong and complicated man. I worshipped him growing up. He taught me about loyalty by example. He had every reason to leave my mom. He stuck with her through all the years of alcoholism, all the fights and then the years that followed where he had to care for her until her death. And then he continued to care for my uncle until he died. More on that topic soon.

Strength, loyalty and redemption. Everyone deserves a second chance. You don't quit on people even when it's hard. That is what together my parents instilled upon me by their example and their deeds. As imperfect and complicated as they were, I couldn't be prouder of my parents.

ROYAL GARDENS
TO BOG ROAD

There you have it. That was Royal Gardens. We lived there until I was fifteen years old. Every day was unsafe. Every day had the potential for trauma. Every day, there was a constant need to be on guard. And it didn't matter if I was inside my apartment or outside in the projects. There wasn't anywhere that was safe or secure.

My friends and I, we found ways to survive. We all made decisions based on what we knew at the time. Some were good. Some not so much. It was all we knew. We didn't have a choice. We survived our childhoods.

What you just read is the difference between PTSD and CPTSD. Prolonged trauma for that many years causes what medical professionals are now calling Complex Post Traumatic Stress Disorder. Whatever you call it, the effects of trauma are the same. It's just a label. But, to the person whose lived it? It's a lot more.

So, that is part of what is in THE BOX.

I mentioned that I have never drank or done drugs. In addition to the moment I mentioned, I have always believed that if I'm sober I can keep myself and those I care about safe. By being in control I can be safe, and keep others safe. Why does that matter so much to me?

Well...before we address that far darker and much more evil thing that lurks in THE BOX, let's stop by my home on Bog Road where I moved to at fifteen years old...

BOG
ROAD

I mentioned my dad took care of my uncle a few pages ago. My uncle fell into a well when he was four years old and was underwater for four minutes. For the rest of his life, he was stuck, mentally, at about eight years old. He needed routines. He needed consistency. He worked at the Rumford Press sweeping floors until he had to retire due to severe depression.

He lived with my grandmother until she died of colon cancer. After my grandmother died, we moved from the projects to my grandmother's house to take care of my uncle.

I was so excited! I was moving out of the projects! I was moving to a house! And, it wasn't going to be long before I had my driver's license! I'd still be able to see my friends in the projects!

This house, our family homestead, was built by my grandfather in 1929. The land it was built on has been in my family since the late 1800's. The original structure was 20 by 24 feet - yes, 480 square feet total plus a front porch. It was a bungalow style home.

My mom was born and died in this very house. So did my uncle. My grandparents raised eight (8) kids in this house. There was no indoor bathroom until the 1950's. There was one small bedroom that had a sheet hanging from the ceiling to divide the boys from the girls, who shared a bed apiece. My grandparents slept in the living room, near the wood stove to keep warm. The house, like many in that time period, had no insulation.

My grandfather built a workshop behind the house. It was covered on the outside with green tar paper. He was good with his hands. We call this building the "Shop."

We moved into the house in the early summer. Well, we didn't all move into the house. As I mentioned, it was small. My parents slept in the living room like my grandparents did. My uncle got the small bedroom (made smaller by the bathroom that was added in the 1950's). His bedroom measured six by eight feet.

My brother and I pitched a tent in the back yard. We lived out there all summer. A kid from the projects was now living at a house with a yard! We were excited to have a place like this to pitch a tent. And we got to live in it all summer! It was awesome! Well, until it got cold or rainy.

Our parents were trying to decide if they could afford to build an addition on the house to make room for us. As I mentioned before, money was tight. As they kept trying to figure out a plan and time passed, the weather was changing, so my brother and I moved into the one car detached garage.

We set up our beds in the garage. We also ran an electrical cord from the house to the garage so we could plug in our electric blankets - our only heat source.

My brother came up with the idea of fixing up the Shop so that he and I could move into it. Why my parents agreed to this I don't recall. My brother and I talk about this every once in a while - we can't figure out why they agreed to this. Read on to gain some insight.

It was a two-room shed. Over time, we put in a new floor. We had to. My brother dropped a tool, an ax I think, and it went right through the rotten floor boards. It was quite old.

We put my grandfather's wood stove in there for heat and managed to get electricity out there too. Never had running water. The shed was about seventy-five feet behind the house. I know because I helped dig the trench for the electrical lines.

I was sixteen and my brother nineteen. We were living in a shed, and it was so much better than living in the projects. My friends would come over and we'd play board games, Dungeons and Dragons and play the Atari 2600 all night long. No parents to tell us to go to sleep. We weren't keeping them up while being loud. We had our own place!

We learned a lot too. One winter night a friend from the projects stayed overnight. I was too tired to load the wood stove before we fell asleep. We had a large outdoor thermometer on one of the walls inside the shed. We woke up and could see our breath as we exhaled. He said, shivering, "I think I'm gonna die!" We looked at the thermometer. It was minus 20 (-20) degrees Fahrenheit. At least we had the electric blanket. Lesson learned.

Another time, the wood stove damper was left open and the stove pipe got so hot it turned bright red. And because we didn't know any better, we hadn't screwed the pipes together and the red-hot pipe fell off! As the Shop filled with smoke, my brother had to grab that red-hot pipe with stove gloves and put it back in place. I don't recall that we ever told our parents about that...

As I mentioned, my mom was sick and we also had to take care of my uncle. When he fell into a very deep depression, things got even more difficult. After all other treatments failed, he needed electric shock therapy, which he got at the Dartmouth Medical Center in NH. He was a complex case.

Daily, I would come home from high school and help both mom and my uncle with their medical needs.

One time, I was helping my uncle get cleaned up. I told him it was time for his shower. He was resistant. I had to break down the process into steps. I suggested he go into the bathroom, get undressed, turn on the water, open the curtain, get into the shower, and then, close the curtain. I assured him I would be right outside the door. I was sixteen years old.

After some time passed, I heard the water turn on and the shower curtain move. I knocked on the door and he didn't respond.

I opened the door and noticed there were no clothes on the floor. I looked in the shower and he was standing under the shower head, water pouring down on him, fully clothed. This was a normal day for me while in high school.

Thankfully, over time the shock therapy and other treatments began to work. He had to have very stringent routines to be healthy. Supper at the same time every day. Bedtime at the same time too. Oh, and he walked miles every day. I mean miles and miles. He'd wave to people. Everyone who lived nearby knew of him.

He loved to eat mixed nuts. He always had Twinkies and Diet Pepsi in the fridge. He loved to watch John Wayne movies. And, when he saw a pudgy baby he'd always say in a cute affectionate way, "Oh, look at you, you fat shlob! Ha ha ha!"

And just as I found my mom's body when she died, I found his dead body in his bedroom. He died of a heart attack when getting up from bed one morning. Just twenty-two months after my mom passed.

Eddie, as he was nicknamed by some of my relatives, told me that because he never married and never had kids, he was worried that he'd be forgotten after he died. Well, Uncle Edward, you have not been forgotten! You will always be part of our affectionate memories.

Although things improved by moving to Bog Road from the projects, my life as a high schooler was not normal. It was hard to try to be a normal teenager, working at the local supermarket, while having to take care of my mom and uncle, all while living in a shed with my brother while he was finding his way too.

My brother and I used to fight a lot about his use of alcohol and pot. I didn't want any of that around me and I was sick of his playing drums while I was trying to sleep. I'm sure I annoyed him too.

He was bigger than me. He was a fighter when he needed to be. He used to torment me like a lot of siblings did. And one time, I grew so angry, I wasn't afraid of him. Oh, and it helped that I had one of those sharp garden rakes in my hands.

I chased him while swinging the garden rake. He ran into the house through the back door, trying to get away from me. I was right behind him swinging the garden rake at him.

He ran past my parents in the living room and ran out the front door. I was right on his heels, garden rake in hand, yelling at him for whatever he had done to me. Another average day, part of growing up in the projects. And part of being brothers I guess. I just chuckled at what my parents must have thought, when our fight ran by them, me yelling at my brother, swinging a garden rake in the house, while they were watching TV.

And then one summer my brother joined the circus. Yes, he literally joined the circus. But, that's his story to tell. And it's an amazing story. My story, my truth, continues here…

RELIGION

My mom was the most devout Catholic person I know. Her connection to God was unmatched. What does it mean to be religious? And why do people choose to be religious? Good questions!

I was baptized and raised Catholic. It was the only thing I knew as a kid. My mom, both when sober and even more so when drunk, taught me all about the Bible and what Catholics believed. I memorized the Lord's Prayer. I read all the stories about Creation, The Flood, Abraham, Joseph, Moses and the Plagues, and David and Goliath among many others. I also had that Catholic guilt that gets instilled into you.

One day, I wanted a candy bar so bad and I didn't have the money for it. I went into Nault's Pharmacy on Loudon Road in Concord and I stole a Three Musketeer's candy bar. As I was walking home with my newly acquired heist, the Catholic guilt set in. I went back to the pharmacy and put the candy bar back on the shelf unopened. That's Catholic guilt. It was a great babysitter!

I told you that my mom was a devout Catholic. But, even she had some limits on the rules of the Catholic Church. For one, she would always tell my brother and I, "There is no one between you and God. You never have to go to confession. You talk right to God. There is no priest who is between you and God." We didn't go to church often. Why? Well as my mother would say, "Our home is our church."

A Catholic friend once said to me about going to church at Christmas and Easter, "You're an ashes and palms Catholic. You only go when they're giving stuff out." Good humor!

I went to kindergarten at the Immaculate Heart of Mary Church on Loudon Road in Concord. I don't remember attending services there as a kid. I'm guessing between my dad working all the time, having one car, and my mom's drinking, it wasn't a top priority.

Ironically, a lot of people in the projects were religious. There was a Jewish guy who'd come to the playground with a button machine maker. He'd help us make those buttons you could pin to your shirt like politicians do. I don't recall what they'd say though. While we were doing that activity he talked about the Jewish faith. I'm not sure I listened a whole lot, but I did like making those buttons!

There were also these prayer groups that would show up at the playground as well. They'd bring those little bibles you could put in your pockets. I remember coming home and showing my mother my new pocket bible. It had a green cover. She looked at it and made sure it was a Christian bible; then she was fine with it.

I had a rosary that my mom hung on the headboard of my bed to keep me safe at night, kind of like a Native American dream catcher. I recall getting a cross necklace. I wore it all the time. It protected me from evil. I felt safer when I was wearing that cross.

When I wore that cross, I felt like God was right next to me. Like he was walking beside me through the projects. It gave me confidence that I could safely get to the public swimming pool and back without getting beat up. Oh, it didn't mean I wouldn't get chased or threatened. But, it did mean I had a better chance of making it home.

When I prayed as a kid before bed, I'd always ask for the same thing, "God give me the strength to endure whatever comes my way tomorrow." Maybe back then I'd replace 'endure' with 'survive.' But, you get the gist.

As I got a little older, say ten, I'd ask questions. And at some point someone asked me to go to a church with them. I don't know the denomination. But they said it was Christian.

My mom said I could go as long as it was Christian. I went to many different churches with many different families. My mom never even asked who I was going with or when I'd be back. Recall, we were unsupervised back then.

Church was odd. A bunch of people all doing the same thing at the same time. There were rules. I knew the Catholic ones. You know; when to stand, when to kneel, when to sit, when to bow your heads and where to look in the book for lyrics to the hymns (songs). But this place was different.

I'm sure the adults in the neighborhood knew that us kids had it rough. We probably needed to be saved and didn't know it. But, these adults knew it and they were kind, friendly and caring. A lot of times, I'd have to use my bike to get to church. Sometimes church with these adults came with hot chocolate and riding in a car. I remember bobbing for Apples at one church function.

There was never a doubt God existed. What was there to doubt? I knew about him ever since I could understand English. We'd watch the TV movies at Christmas and Easter - Ben Hur, Moses, Jesus and the like. My mother loved these shows. She'd cry while watching them. Especially movies about Jesus' resurrection.

I remember my mom telling me that when she was a child the Virgin Mary came to her in a field. I don't remember all the details except that Mary told my mom she'd return before my mom was about to die. Seemed kind of scary to me. To know you're about to die, that is. But my mother believed what she told me, and I never questioned it. Still don't.

Having a faith in something that is so powerful and so real is a wonderful thing. Everything is going to be okay. God cares for you. God will guide you. God watches over you.

We had religious objects all through our apartment in the projects. Crosses, palms, pictures of the Pope and Jesus on the cross. My mom had holy water in a bottle on a shelf near the clock. During bad thunderstorms, she would open the bottle, dip her finger in and make the sign of the cross on the windows to keep us safe. Despite all the challenges in my childhood, the one thing that was a constant, was God.

God's word was delivered through representatives right here on earth. They went by many titles: priest, pastor, deacon, bishop, reverend, elder, abbot, and chaplain, among many others. As a child, these titles put me in awe. Like the Pope, they were representatives of God. They knew what God expects of us. If we don't listen to these representatives of the Lord, the all-knowing, all-powerful, righteous and merciful God will punish us. You've heard the phrase, "God will strike you down with lightning!" I grew up believing that with all my heart and soul.

ERNEST HAROLD "RUSTY" PETTIS JR

Here we are, finally, at THE BOX. For 30 years, my mind has been working day and night nonstop to keep me from opening THE BOX.

At this point in my life, after injuring my back at forty years old, I've spent several years in constant chronic pain. My mind is exhausted.

Now, it makes more sense why I was thinking that the only way to end my pain was to die by suicide. Chronic pain can be crushing on the mind. My mind made the decision for me that it could no longer deal with both the physical pain and keeping THE BOX closed any longer. The only solution was to end my life. Thankfully, I got help before I executed the plan.

And again, if you're having suicidal thoughts right now - stop reading and dial 988. Good people will be there to help you.

It was in this moment, at 3:00 am during a brutal night terror, when THE BOX opened and the name Ernest Harold "Rusty" Pettis Jr came out. You couldn't have written a better name for a character in a horror movie.

Who was Rusty? Well, he was a kind man. He taught me things. He paid attention to me when others didn't. I wasn't invisible around him. He would tell me I mattered. He made time for me. He told me that God loved me. And he should know, since he was one of God's representatives. He had reddish hair and a red beard. Oh yeah, and he was also a pedophile priest. My pedophile priest.

Now, I'm not going to sit here and sugar coat this. I'm no longer a scared and frightened child but sometimes PTSD triggers can bring that child out. What I find interesting now that I've gotten healthier is that people like to use soft terms when describing the actions of a pedophile like; he touched him inappropriately; he molested him; he sexually abused him.

Why? Because it makes people uncomfortable to use the correct term - RAPE.

In fact, I myself couldn't say the word, RAPE, for years even in therapy. I wasn't able to. I didn't want it to be true. But, no matter how I described it, how I avoided the word - the correct term is RAPE.

In every sense of the word. Everything you connote with the word RAPE. It happened. It happened to me when I was about eleven or twelve years old. On and off, for about a year, maybe a year and a half.

Rusty manipulated me. He groomed me. He used God to control me. He threatened me if I told anyone. He stole my childhood, tortured my mind and RAPED my very soul.

I have no intention of getting into the description of what the RAPE was like. You know. You can use your imagination.

I will tell you how this started. After going to this church with a friend and his family, Rusty got a liking for me. He made me feel visible. Nice thoughtful words. And after a while, I was special to him. So much so, I was invited to a cabin on a lake during the winter to go snowmobiling with the church group.

After a fun day with others, on the lake and in the snow, it was time to go to sleep. I slept in my sleeping bag right next to the wood stove in the cottage to keep warm. Rusty slept right next to me. He reached into my sleeping bag while I was laying on my stomach to rub my back to keep me "warm." Then as he rubbed my back his hand slid into and under my underwear. I froze.

He pulled his hand out quickly. I thought it must have been an accident at first. I then tried to roll away. He didn't let me. This time his hand went into my underpants again and to this day I can feel his fingers exploring; the more I tried to pull away, the tighter his grip became; the more his fingers became invasive, trying to reach under me and to the front, the more frightened I became. My childhood innocence was destroyed that night.

So, how does a child get controlled by a pedophile priest? Well, it starts with them knowing you're easy prey. I've already shared what my childhood was like. We grew up unsupervised. We had too much freedom. Oh right, but we had God protecting us. Can you hear my eyes rolling?

Now, I'm going to describe this using the words I know now. At the age I was, when this happened, I wouldn't know to describe things using the vocabulary I have today.

In fact, back then I was numb. Probably couldn't say anything anyway. But unfortunately, it took me 30 years to open THE BOX. To start to heal my soul.

By far the absolute worst things Rusty did were mental torture. I mean, he was a man of God. A full-on representative of the Lord himself. When he was in pedophile mode he would subtly threaten me with comments like, "God is all knowing," implying that if I told anyone, God would know and Rusty would find out and I or my family would be harmed.

Here's another one, "It's God's will." So, according to Rusty, it was God's will to RAPE a child. But, what did I know? I had no reason not to believe. My mother suffered all the time, and she was unflinching in her belief in God. Maybe this was in fact God's will? Maybe I should stop resisting? Maybe I should accept my fate? After all, God doesn't make mistakes.

Rusty was good at emotional manipulation. He gave me hugs when he wanted to. When I wanted one, he wouldn't. One minute he was caring, kind, thoughtful and priestly. But, if I resisted, hesitated, or tried to do anything but what he wanted, there was this simmering anger under the surface.

You know the kind of anger, like God was pissed off. I knew the stories of the Old Testament. I knew what that angry vengeful God could do.

Over time I learned to not feel. I learned to shut down my body when he touched me. I learned that if I didn't resist whatever was going to happen would end quicker and hurt less. I practiced what I always knew, you obey God and God's representatives on earth.

There was no way to end this horror story. If I told anyone, they could be punished by God. I would be punished by God.

The adults in my life failed me. The more I resisted going to church, any church, the more the adults in my life saw a kid from the projects, with an alcoholic mother and an absent father, who needed the Lord to save him. They fed me to a pedophile and they didn't even know it.

I don't blame any of them. In fact, I still know and love many of them. They were trying to do right by me. Rusty is the sole person to blame.

You're probably wondering how this ended?

When my mother was in one of her comas, I thought it was my fault. That I must have thought something bad about Rusty. That God chose to put my mother in a coma to punish me. I went back to Rusty on my bicycle thinking I could make it right and save my mom.

That's how brainwashed I was. That's how much control he had over me. That's how much I loved my mom. I would go back and submit to his abuse one more time.

That was a rational thought. That was a logical action. That was what I needed to do to save my mom. After all, it was my fault she laid in a coma.

But after I left Rusty, when I was riding my bike home, I shouted and yelled at God, "I don't care if you strike me down with lightning! I'm never going back there again!" That was the last time I've ever spoken to God. And it was the last time I ever saw Rusty in person.

That was when THE BOX was created, closed, chained shut and locked. My mind would protect me from its contents for over thirty years. For thirty plus years the pain surfaced occasionally as PTSD symptoms, but it took that long for me to start climbing from THE BOX to mountaintop of healing.

I have told you my story. Now you know the origin of my traumas. What follows now is that journey up the mountain to healing. You will read about various methods I tried to heal my mind, body and soul, because I want to encourage you to try new things if you have trauma to overcome. The first step on my journey was Exposure Therapy.

Chapter 6

CONFRONTING THE PAST

EXPOSURE THERAPY

When I finally was able to talk to Steve during therapy, I blurted out something like, "Tell me how to fix me. I don't want to feel like this anymore." See, Rusty stole my childhood and decades of my adult life - the rest of my life was going to be mine! I was determined that Rusty was not going to win. It's my life - Rusty doesn't get to win! This became my rallying cry, "Rusty Doesn't Get To Win!"

Steve was my guide. Steve helped me process the chaos in my mind. He'd ask questions, make observations, and teach me about techniques I could choose to try.

The primary approach that has consistently worked for me is Exposure Therapy. When Steve first introduced me to the concept he described it like this:

"Let's say you're afraid to ride elevators. So, go ride the elevator fifty times. At some point, you'll realize nothing bad is going to happen and you'll get bored of doing it."

For me, coming out of 5 West (in-patient behavioral health), I couldn't pass a church, any church, without being triggered. My hands would grip the steering wheel, white-knuckling it! DANGER! DANGER! My heart raced! BAD THINGS HAPPEN THERE! I'd be sweating. My breathing would shallow. Fight or flight!

I began to try this new Exposure Therapy technique. At first, I would drive by a church. Then drive by the church a couple of times a day. Once I had the repetition and reassurance that nothing bad happened, I tried to walk by a church.

I was working downtown at the time. I'd take my lunch break and go for a walk, always planning those walks to go by a church. I was making really good progress the more I repeated this. Steve was right, just like he said about the elevator. This was becoming no big deal.

Then it happened. I was walking by a church and the front door opened and out walked a priest. Full on panic. DANGER DANGER DANGER! RUN! RUN! My mind screamed at me. I quickened my pace and got away from the priest and the church. I began to hyperventilate. Panic set in. Heart pounding, lungs quickened. Sweat poured off me. Back to Steve I went...

"You lied to me! You said that I'd be safe!" Steve always handled those moments well. He'd ask me things like - "Why did you feel unsafe? Describe for me the bad thing that happened." Over a long time, it started to become clearer.

All the bad things that were happening, were happening in my mind. Oh, they absolutely were real. But Steve's point was also true. Nothing bad physically happened to me. My brain triggered fight or flight because it thought the priest was going to harm me. Why? Because a priest did harm me! And my PTSD mind doesn't separate the past from the present.

Eventually, I went back to my walks by the churches.

What happened with the priest coming out of the church was a major setback in my mind. I felt like I was starting this Exposure Therapy with churches all over again. But, I wasn't. I didn't go back to driving by churches like I had started. I was still okay with walking by one.

As time went on, I would stop in front of the church and just stand there. I would time myself to see long I could stand there before fight or flight kicked in. I did this for long time. It was a lot for me to do. But, I kept at it.

I think another term for this approach is also called Desensitization. It's kind of like Exposure Therapy where you do something over and over in a safe and controlled way. But, I like that term better because I'm just taking it in and desensitizing to it at a pace that works for me.

The next step was to walk to up the steps of the church. For whatever reason, this step was a little easier than the ones before it. I didn't question why. After I got to this point, my family took a trip to Old Quebec just east of Montreal, Canada. We were doing all the touristy things. My boys were young. And they saw a cool old church - one you might see in the movies. They wanted to go inside. But, I couldn't go in.

I stood outside and watched my boys and their mother go into the church. Then the PTSD kicked in. "Your children are in DANGER! It is not safe for them to be in the church! Bad things happen in churches!" I was in such a panic after they went in, I called Steve from Canada.

As I talked to Steve, he broke things down for me. He asked me, "What do you see?" I'm sure I answered with something like, "Evil." He then went on to remind me that an architect designed the building. And from that perspective, what did I see?

By the time we finished talking, I had broken down the building in my head into stone, wood and metal. It was no longer a church. It was just another historical building in Old Quebec. And with that change in thinking, I found a way to walk into a church.

Oh, I was anxious, for sure. No doubt. But, I did it. I did it, because in my head, I needed to keep my family safe - especially my kids. They were with their mother. But I needed to keep them safe. All of them!

I kept reminding myself this was a tourist site, a historical building, a structure made of rocks, wood and metal. Even with all that progress, that night PTSD kicked in, and the church resurfaced in my nightmares. But, I was okay with that. I had done something I thought wasn't possible. I walked into a church and I was safe. My family was safe. My kids were safe.

Today, I limit going to churches generally to weddings and funerals. Make no mistake, I'm absolutely still triggered. I will likely have nightmares following being in a church.

Sometimes the nightmares go on for a couple of weeks. But, I also know that they will stop. I choose to accept the possibility of nightmares instead of fear them. That way, I can choose to participate in important events in people's lives and be there for them during their weddings and support and encourage them when they lose a loved one.

What I learned

What to expect if you try exposure therapy:

- *Start small - I began just driving by churches, not going inside*
- *Expect setbacks - the priest coming out of the church felt like starting over, but I wasn't really back to square one*
- *Have a support system - I called Steve from Canada when I panicked*
- *Set your own pace - no one should push you faster than you're ready to go*
- *Celebrate small victories - each step forward matters, even if it seems tiny*

The key is controlled, gradual exposure in safe environments. Never let anyone pressure you into exposure that feels unsafe or too fast.

ADAM, DOCTOR OF OSTEOPATHIC MEDICINE

Part 3

Now let's go back in time a bit; I'm three years into PTSD treatments and the trauma is very much in the way of healing my physical back injury. And, now that you know the sources of my trauma and how it occurred over years it's probably starting to make more sense why being touched was such a trigger. It happened with my first physical therapist in PT before I even knew I had PTSD. And it is getting in the way of being treated by Adam now. So, Adam and I had to come up with a plan.

But first, we had to rebuild trust again. Remember that book that was in the waiting room? You know the one, it triggered me and I lost trust with Adam before I even met him? Well it's back.

Adam was moving his office across the hall. I was nervous about the new location. What did the office look like? Would I be safe there? What if something bad happened, how could I leave? Where were the exits? And yes, would that book still be in his new waiting room?

Oh right! That book. Some people call it The Bible. Why there was a Bible in a doctor's office waiting room, who knows? For me, it was a major trigger. Depending on PTSD symptoms, I struggled to be in a church, near a priest or the symbols of religion and a Bible was just another one of those symbols.

So, when Adam moved across the hall, I asked him if the Bible was in the new waiting room. He told me he looked throughout the waiting room and assured me that it wasn't there.

I agreed to meet him after the practice closed for the day, so he could give me a tour to avoid any new triggers from the new location. I got there a few minutes early to make sure the Bible was gone. I looked around the new waiting room before Adam arrived. So far so good.

Then I walked across the hall to where his old office and waiting room were. The door was closed and locked to the old waiting room. But, there was a built-in coat rack outside the waiting room. Above the pole and hangers there was a shelf for hats and stuff. On top of that shelf was the Bible. The SAME BIBLE! I lost it. BOOM – P T S D!

By the time Adam arrived a few minutes later, I was in a full-on panic attack. I couldn't believe he lied to me. I couldn't believe he'd harm me like that. I was hyperventilating and couldn't catch my breath. He kept asking me what was wrong and I couldn't talk. I walked him across the hall and pointed to the Bible. He understood.

He asked me to come in to his new office and assured me there would be no Bibles in there. He would get me away from this Bible if I went with him. I followed him. He unlocked the door and asked my permission every step of the way as he worked to get me into a treatment room. I'm sure he thought four walls with a closed door would feel safer for me. He was right and it did.

By this point, I probably had a flashback and I may have passed out. Adam did everything right. He was patient, kind, supportive, and understanding. He gave me the room I needed and the safe space to work through the PTSD symptoms.

He reassured me in calming tones that I was safe. He reassured me that if I wanted to leave he wouldn't stop me and followed it with, "But I don't want you to leave. I'd like to work through this with you." I knew if I left before we resolved this major violation of trust, I'd never come back. To be clear, Adam did nothing wrong. My PTSD mind just told me he did.

Once I could talk and the symptoms had subsided some, we talked through what happened. He didn't know the Bible was there. And he assured me, if I chose to come back the Bible wouldn't be there anymore.

At the next appointment, the Bible was gone. Yup! I checked. And I never asked Adam where the Bible went. I was just glad it was gone.

This is how Adam and I worked together. Whenever there was a perceived violation of trust – I'd freak out or, more accurately, PTSD symptoms surfaced – and each time, Adam was consistent, reassuring, and understanding. He always gave me the space to work through the PTSD symptoms in a safe, healthy and reassuring way.

I was a lot to handle in those appointments. Neither one of us knew when or how PTSD symptoms would come out. But, as we built trust in each other, it became more predictable, which was reassuring for the both of us.

We came up with a plan to help me deal with the fear of being touched. After all, how was Adam going to help me with the physical issues, if I wouldn't let him touch me. So, we also started practicing Exposure Therapy.

He brought in a medical text book and we'd sit next to each other on the exam table. Adam would open the book and he'd explain to me all about how the human muscles and skeletal system works. How everything is connected and why pain in one area could be a tight muscle in another area. I think that was called referred pain. And, why tight muscles could cause limping or not being able to bend your back normally. We discussed things in great detail.

Over time, we began to bring the things in the textbook out into practice. He'd show me the muscle in the book, tell me its function and then ask for permission to show me on my body where that muscle is. We ran into a new trigger.

It turns out being touched through my shirt was a major trigger. So was being touched by a stethoscope through my shirt. Blood pressure cuff over my sleeve, yep.

Eventually I learned it is much easier for me to just take off my shirt before being touched. Doing so gets rid of the feeling of Rusty sliding his hands over and under my clothing.

To this very day my current PCP, prior to listening to my heart/lungs, always remembers to let me take my shirt off. It's a simple solution to avoid time consuming, emotionally draining and brutal triggers. I've also learned that an expected safe hug isn't a trigger. Odd how the PTSD mind works. One type of touch is safe; another is a direct connection to the traumatic past.

Adam would tell me about a muscle and how it was likely causing back pain. He would use his hands and show me the muscle on my back. He would ask me to move and arm or a leg while he held his hand on my back muscle so I could feel its movements. Over time, I would repeat the same thing on his back. I was beginning to understand my body, and my body was beginning to relax a bit.

I was beginning to understand that the trauma, the RAPE, was stored in the muscles of my body. The more Adam and I repeated the process over the weeks and months that followed, the less anxious I was. I wasn't triggered as often. Exposure Therapy was working once again.

Adam taught me about my body from head to toe, front and back. The more he taught me, the more I started understanding that my trauma was in fact getting in the way of my healing. I was tense. My muscles were like armor protecting me from being touched. Always on alert for fight or flight. Never relaxing. Those tight muscles worsened the pain.

During this process with Adam, I was also seeing Steve each week. Steve and I would process the emotional and psychological PTSD issues I may have had when Adam worked with me. And then at my next appointment with Adam, he and I would do something more physically, and Steve would help me process it a short time later. Wash, rinse, repeat, so to speak.

What was happening here, was that Adam was teaching me and then I'd explain to Steve what I learned. That process of in-and-out in the brain, helped me rethink my trauma in a more clinical light. Everything is just a body part, in a way. It wasn't trauma of the past. It was the human body.

As time went on, my pain was decreasing. Not because of meds, but because this amazing process we created was working. I felt safe with Adam (still do). His touch is safe, clinical and caring. His wasn't the touch of a pedophile that my PTSD mind freaks out about. I began to know the difference. Safe touch vs. evil touch. The more I relaxed, the less pain I had, the more Adam was able to help me with the pain in my back.

My back injuries were as real as anyone else's. What I learned from this process is that trauma, anxiety, fear and triggers can exacerbate the pain.

If without trauma my back pain from the soccer injury was a seven (7) on the pain scale, my trauma exacerbated the pain and made it a ten (10). Understanding this dynamic was a breakthrough for me.

When Adam and I concluded this process, we celebrated! We did what I called a Final Exam where I shared with Adam everything I had learned and we marveled at how little of the anxiety came out.

At the end of our doctor and patient relationship, we began our friendship. Adam is and remains one of my closest friends on the planet.

What I learned

Advocating for yourself in medical settings became essential to my healing:

- *Always speak up when something doesn't feel right (like that Bible trigger)*
- *Ask doctors to explain their approach and why they think it will help*
- *Don't be afraid to request modifications (like removing my shirt instead of being touched through clothing)*
- *Bring an advocate with you if needed*
- *Remember that you can pause or stop any treatment that feels unsafe*
- *Good doctors, like Adam, will work with your triggers and limitations*
- *It's okay to "fire" providers who don't listen or make you feel unsafe - Keep a written list of your triggers and needs to share with new providers*

Building trust with medical providers takes time after trauma, and that's completely normal. The right providers will be patient with your healing process.

THE BOX OPENS
UNEXPECTEDLY

Long before THE BOX allowed me to remember the memory you'll read about next, I was struggling with body issues related to being RAPED. I remember asking doctors during my physicals, 'If I was in a locker room would people be able to tell I was raped?" I cried asking the question every time.

Recall, locker rooms are triggers. My PTSD would scream at me, "Every man is a threat and every penis is a weapon." It wasn't a place I could go. Especially after PTSD surfaced.

While I'd been in locker room during gym class in grade school prior to PTSD coming out, I never played sports in high school; I was never in the military; I was never exposed to public showers as a child. There was no nudity in my home.

When talking to Steve about this and trying to figure out how to handle this body dysmorphia, we talked about things I thought were caused by Rusty.

I have a scar on my penis. I talked to Steve about it. I then talked to my doctor about it. During my annual physical, I showed the scar to my doctor too, so he'd understand what Rusty did to me. The doc, multiple doctors over time, since I needed a lot of reassurance, told me it was a circumcision scar and had nothing to do with Rusty. My PTSD twelve-year-old self didn't believe them. I kept asking. The answers were always the same. So, why wouldn't the scared child believe them? Why did I need to keep asking?

Then I was asking, "But what about this line that appears on my scrotum sometimes? Rusty did that!" Well, I learned that that is the scrotal raphe or sometimes called the perineal raphe. Every guy has that. Depending on skin pigmentation, some are more visible than others. It didn't come from Rusty. "Not true!" Screamed the scared twelve-year-old child. "Rusty did that to me too!"

But I was being told by doctor after doctor that all these things I thought were caused by Rusty were in fact normal things that males have. It's frustrating sometimes. As an adult, I'm wondering, if all that is true that the doctors are telling me, why does my mind get stuck? Why can't I convince the scared twelve-year-old child hiding in THE BOX that all this is normal and not associated with Rusty?

During one of these frustrated moments, Steve asked me what I thought would work? You know, to deal with the body dysmorphia. To convince myself and the scared twelve-year-old boy that my body was the same as other males.

I replied, "The Elevator! You said, if I was scared of the elevator and rode the elevator fifty times, at some point I'd no longer be afraid and I'd get bored with it." He agreed he said that. Then I said, and I laughed at the absurdity of it: "Let's just line up 100 guys and I'll go down the line, look at each one and at some point, it'll register that we are all the same and I'll get bored with it. Problem solved." We both laughed because we knew that wasn't going to happen.

But, Steve assured me that there was a lot of truth to it being a solution. Instead of being told by authority figures that my body was normal, I could see for myself. The traumatized twelve-year-old could see and be reassured and feel safe.

Well, we never lined up a hundred guys, but as it turns out I was correct, I needed to convince the frightened kid that his body was the same as others'.

That twelve-year-old was the one we were really talking to, after all. And, unexpectedly, THE BOX opened up, and let me and all those helping me know why the kid was so stuck on his body not being normal. Not being the same. This was such a big issue that I just couldn't find a way to resolve it until the following happened:

I'm driving down Gully Hill in Concord on my way home. I'm behind the public bus, that I think they call the CAT (Concord Area Transit). The bus is wrapped in an advertisement. It reads, "Making a Difference in Our Community." We stop for a red light at the bottom of Gully Hill. That's when my mind EXPLODED!

Making a Difference in our Community
Making a Difference in our Community
Making a Difference in our Community
Making a Difference
Making a Difference
Making a Difference
Difference
Difference
Difference
DIFFERENT

Memories came flooding back!
I'm different! I'm different! I'M DIFFERENT!

I remembered new details. So far, my mind had protected me from remembering all the contents of THE BOX. Throughout my healing journey, I learned my mind would feed me details whenever it thought I was ready to handle them. This was such a day.

I raced home as fast as I could. I ran from my car and into my house, fell on the floor. I was hyperventilating, crying, sobbing - I'M DIFFERENT!

I was back to being a scared twelve-year-old kid in every way. I was transported to my childhood when I was examined by a priest, God's representative, and felt like God himself told me I was different.

Rusty, acting like a concerned pastoral "doctor" and in his priestly role, asked me to drop my pants so he could see how I was developing puberty-wise. Creep!

At twelve years old. Puberty. The most uncomfortable, awkward and confusing period for anyone irrespective of trauma. A time period when our bodies change and during part of the most formative years of our developing minds. He was about to imprint scars on my mind that decades later, I was struggling to work through.

When my pants were down, he looked intently at my crotch. I was nervous. Sweating. It was awkward. Then he looked up at me and he reassuringly said, "Now, I see why God sent you to me. You are different. I can help you with that."

My blood boils when I think of that moment. At twelve years old, I had God tell me my genitals were different. And God's representative was going to help me make them normal. Rusty used that to gain access to my body. He used that to manipulate me. He used that to control me.

I had just been told, that only God could make me normal and God sent Rusty to help make me normal. Rusty's touch was going to heal me from being different!?!

What the absolute fuck had happened? Who does that to a twelve-year-old kid? What evil lived inside that man? That he would tell an adolescent, going through the biggest physical changes we do as human beings, that God said their genitals were different.

That act of evil was far worse for me than the physical RAPE. It haunted me through the rest of puberty even after I walked away from Rusty and the Church. That twelve-year-old still raises its head to this day, fearing that there is something wrong with my body. The medical term I believe is body dysmorphia.

No matter how many times doctors would reassure me that everything is normal, that moment still haunts my nightmares. That scared child still lives in my mind and in my soul. That imprint in the most formative years of my life can't just be erased. It needs to be re-written.

I've tried so many things to work through that issue. To finally put it to rest. To heal that part of my soul. I've talked to friends, deep conversations, sometimes awkward conversations. But, we try to help each other. Turns out that all of us worry about something in that area of our body or at least did at some point in our lives. At some point, we get to acceptance - it is what it is, so to speak.

BILL, UROLOGIST

This is where my urologist, Bill, comes in. Much like my time with Adam, Bill and I set up a routine and a plan. The idea here was that we were going to essentially talk to the twelve-year-old part of my brain and show through logic that I am not different, not abnormal, not flawed.

We took the approach that we would talk as if I was a scared twelve-year-old boy who had lots of questions. We would deal with every question, even if as an adult I knew the answer. We would be systematic about it. We would try to rewrite the memories.

I would make a list of things that came up in nightmares or PTSD flashbacks related to my twelve-year-old mind telling me I'm different. Bill, like Adam, brought in one of his medical textbooks from college to our appointments.

Bill pulled up an old MRI on the computer from a scan I had of my lower back and hips that included the region we were discussing. He compared the MRI images to the pictures in the text book. Piece by piece, we broke down every part of the male anatomy. Piece by piece, he showed me that my body matched the text book.

Even in these moments of trying to dispel the evil that happened, humor is useful and happened many times. Bill said, "Now, here is the prostrate. This is what the textbook says it should look like and this is yours in the MRI. These ARE different. You have an enlarged prostate. Welcome to your fifty's!" We both laughed. That was something I understood, and it helped.

In essence, we were trying to retrain the brain with objective, logical and factual evidence that things are not different. As Steve, my PCP, Adam and other docs have said to me over and over, "If you can urinate and procreate, everything is working fine and is normal." That's the bottom line.

I made a lot of good progress with Bill. One moment sticks out for me. At one appointment, Bill brought in a piece of paper with five pictures on it. It was the Tanner Stages of physical development in children, adolescents and adults. In this case, we focused on the male genitalia.

I started to cry. An answer was clear in front of me. The pictures were lined up from left to right, child to adulthood. I was more on the left side of the pictures at twelve years old. Rusty was on the far right as an adult. He was around 30 years old when he RAPED me.

I was in fact "different" at twelve years old. I was different from my adult rapist. But, I was not different from where I should have been as a child. I was the same as other children around my age. Working with Bill taught me that healing sometimes means revisiting the same issue from different angles until you find the approach that works.

What I hope you take away from this is that, on your journey, you should keep trying things. Keep poking at the thing that haunts you. It may not be quick to find an answer, but an answer may surface for you. Be open to approaches you haven't tried. Try the things you think won't work. They just might.

All this exposure and desensitization therapy was a big part of what I needed to continue to heal my soul. I am far healthier on this topic. It has become a back burner issue. I know the twelve-year-old doubts will surface from time to time and this will continue this part of my journey. But, it is healing.

Things make more sense. My triggers on this topic are far fewer and farther between and much less intense. It is because of those of you that heard my story and invested your time, love and compassion in me. I am forever grateful.

Chapter 7

FINDING NEW PATHS

I'M FIFTY YEARS OLD!

When I turned fifty years old, I was eight years into my PTSD healing. I was doing pretty well by now – well enough that I decided to try to do something I knew would be triggering. I went down to visit one of the local CrossFit (CF) gyms. I chose this gym because on their website the owner posted about his struggles with PTSD (military) and how CrossFit changed his life for the better. It helped him to be healthier.

I walked in unannounced. the owner was in there by himself. I told him why I was interested in CF. I told him that I saw he had PTSD on the website and that I had it too.

I couldn't believe I chose to trust someone with those four letters on day one. After the owner and I set up the onboarding process and set a date and time to meet, I left and marveled at how far I had already come in my healing.

It turned out that there were a lot of triggers, expected and unexpected, at the gym. Each time I got triggered, the owner did everything he could to help me manage it. He even spoke to my doctors, Steve and Adam, for guidance on how to help me.

After I finished all the onboarding, I was scared to go into a class. I thought it would be too much for me. The owner encouraged me to give it a shot. I finally agreed.

When I got into a class, I struggled. Not from day one. But, things started happening. Memories. Details from the past. The facility reminded me of a basement. Bad things happened to me in a basement.

When this happened, I would go into a room in the back, so I didn't disrupt the class. I also didn't want anyone to see me triggered.

One of the other coaches, who didn't know I had PTSD, came back on his own accord to check on me and I jumped up, startled. He opened his arms and absorbed me in a hug as I jumped up. He hung on to me until I started to settle down. I felt safe. I couldn't believe it, but somehow I felt safe.

At the gym over time, my triggers became more frequent and more intense, to the point that once a coach called 911 because I was having a panic attack and was having difficulty communicating.

That's when I met the owner of another CrossFit gym in town. He happened to also be a firefighter and showed up as part of the 911 response. A short time later, it made sense for me to switch gyms.

The owner of the first gym and I parted ways. He helped me on my journey more than he likely knows. He went all in and did the best he could. To this day, I respect him a great deal.

When I arrived at the new CrossFit gym, I was nervous. Would I be triggered here too? I talked to the owner of the second gym. I reminded him how he and I had previously met. We talked about whether or not this gym would be a good fit for me and we agreed to give it a go. It turned out to be the perfect change.

Not only did he know I had PTSD, but he was great about not sharing it. We had an unspoken code. He'd give me hints on how to handle things. He always did so discreetly. And he'd either call or text me to check in once and a while.

Not only that, but lo and behold, one of the coaches from the first gym, was also going to this CrossFit gym too! You couldn't have planned this transition any better! He was my additional safety net at the new gym.

He had already seen me having a panic attack at the other gym. I already felt safe with him. He never asked me questions. He would smile, wink or do something to let me know - he knew - and he had my back.

The transition wasn't perfect. I had new triggers. Rusty, my abuser, had red hair and a beard. Some people at this gym had red hair or beards. During a few winter months, I ended up growing a beard myself as a way to desensitize to it. It's just facial hair, I tried to convince myself. That trigger isn't as intense now as it used to be. Growing my own beard was another form of Exposure Therapy and desensitization that worked.

I've been at the 2nd CrossFit gym now for a few years. I've worked through a lot of PTSD triggers. I've gotten to know a lot of great people. It's a great community! Committing to a CrossFit habit is one of the best decisions I've made in regard to my journey up to the mountain top of healing.

What I learned

What I learned about returning to physical activities with PTSD:

- *Start with facilities that have trauma-informed staff if possible*
- *Visit during off-peak hours initially to reduce overwhelm*
- *Identify your exit routes and safe spaces before starting activities*
- *Don't be afraid to take breaks or step away when triggered*
- *Find one person there who knows about your PTSD and can be your safety contact*
- *Accept that some days will be harder than others - that's not failure*
- *Consider telling instructors/coaches about specific triggers (like red hair/beards for me)*

Having owner and the second gym owner know about my PTSD made all the difference. I didn't have to explain my reactions in the moment - they just supported me.

BIOLOGICAL
DECODING

In 2018, I went with some family and friends to Costa Rica. As a group we decided to hire massage therapists to come to our Airbnb and do massages outside on the deck in the evening overlooking the ocean. The therapists were both male and female. As it happened, I ended up with the male. His name was Matias.

As you can imagine, the thought of being touched by a guy was triggering for me. Again, I convinced myself I could do this. I'd been working hard at dealing with my triggers. This was a good opportunity to see how healthy I'd become. After all, we were all together in the same house. I wasn't alone and I wasn't twelve years old anymore. This was good way to test myself in a healthy, controlled and safe way.

Matias was a tall guy. He was very kind. He had this way about him that was reassuring. Almost mystical in a calming sort of way. He'd put his hands together under his chin and do a short bow when he greeted you. His first language is Spanish but he speaks English well. 99% of the massage went great.

Oh, you thought it was easy? Would I be mentioning it in this book if nothing had happened?

At one point, his hand placement made me jump. Matias did absolutely everything right. This wasn't about Matias, or the location of his hand; everything was totally appropriate. This was about Rusty, THE BOX, PTSD and my triggers.

Matias didn't know I had PTSD. He apologized for startling me. I'm sure I said something about it being okay and no big deal. That of course was despite my mind going into overdrive and catastrophizing that I could never be healthy. "This proves it! I'll never feel safe! I'll always be triggered! Every man is a threat and every penis is a weapon! I'm not safe anywhere in the world! What's the point of trying!?!" Yup! Just jumped from 'A' to 'Z' again! And I skipped all twenty-four letters in between!

Then in 2020, I returned to Costa Rica with a much larger group of family and friends. I think we had nearly thirty people on this trip. We rented two large Airbnb's. A large group wanted to get massages.

Now, in the years since I was first in Costa Rica, I continued to find ways to heal. This time, I was sure I could try to do a massage again and be healthy. And it turned out that Matias was one of the massage therapists who was coming. This time I chose Matias. I was going to face my trigger head on.

Matias remembered me. Why wouldn't he? A PTSD-level startle is probably hard to forget. I'm sure it doesn't happen often, or at least I hope it doesn't.

Everything about the massage went perfectly. I was not triggered. I did not startle. I succeeded in overcoming a fear!

After I got dressed, Matias came back into the room, and I started to cry. We talked about how I was triggered last time. He told me he remembered. I told him why. I told him what happened to me. He hugged me. I felt safe. Then he asked me to lay on the table again.

Matias is also a "healer." I don't know what type or where he trained. But, I knew I could trust him. He put his hand on my abdomen and asked me to close my eyes. He was attempting to heal me. I could hear his other hand's wrist and fingers snapping, maybe his arm was waving too. Then I could feel warmth in my abdomen. I imagined that there was a light between his hand and my abdomen. Something was happening that I didn't understand.

When he was done, Matias told me I needed more healing and he wanted to help me. Unfortunately, I wasn't going to be in Costa Rica much longer. He asked me if we could meet somewhere before I left. So, I texted him later and told him that I would be at a restaurant with family later in the evening. Matias showed up with healing oils.

We went through a book to determine what fit my healing needs based on my specific trauma and he put the different oils in a dropper to create a mixture that matched my trauma and told me how many drops to put on my tongue and how often. He gave me the list of ingredients so I could look it up on the internet to be sure it was all healthy and I wasn't allergic to anything. He wrote everything down for me. In fact, I still have the paper he gave me.

When I got back home, I called Adam and he concurred all the ingredients were safe and some of them were used in the US as well.

I was nearing the point that I'd try just about anything to end the PTSD symptoms. I just wanted to feel safe *all the time*. I wanted the hypervigilance to stop. I wanted to sleep without any nightmares. I wanted to heal my soul.

I used the dropper just as Matias told me. Honestly, I don't know for sure if it helped. But psychologically, it gave me hope. I chose to try something I hadn't tried before and I chose to trust Matias, and I was proud of those choices.

Here was this guy in Costa Rica, who heard my story and did what he could to help me. He didn't ask for any money. He stayed in contact with me. To this day, we still are in contact. He is my friend. My brother.

At some point Matias suggested that I try Biological Decoding. He said that his brother, Nico, who lives in Argentina, is a Biological Decoder and that if I wanted to try it, he'd reach out to his brother and get us connected. I agreed.

I then went on to research what biological decoding is and how it works. There was not much available on the topic. Even the internet was coming up short.

I finally found a book on Amazon that touched on the topic. I bought it and quickly read it from cover to cover. I needed to understand what I was about to do - so that I'd feel safe.

Nico and I talked by phone. His English isn't as good as his brother's. A lot of humor arose because of that. We laughed a lot as a result of our occasional inability to communicate clearly. But his English was way better than my non-existent Spanish. We talked about how biological decoding would work. He preferred to do biological decoding in person. But, given the geography between us, we agreed to use FaceTime.

Nico raised concerns about PTSD and how I might pass out during sessions with him. He told me that in fact, when Nico went through biological decoding as a patient, he had fainted. The sessions could be intense. He wanted to be sure I had someone there with me. I didn't.

But I had a friend who lived close by. So, I gave Nico his phone number and alerted my friend. This agreement worked for both of us. I wanted to heal and Nico wanted to help and he wanted to make sure I was safe. Trust was building between us.

I'm sure you're wondering what could possibly cause me to pass out while doing talk therapy with a guy 6,000 miles away on FaceTime. You and me both!

I'm not going to share the details of the sessions because part of how they work is that you don't know what's going to be talked about nor the imagery you picture in your mind. What I will share is that each session went on for four to six hours straight. I would describe it as intense talk and imagery therapy. You-are-not-let-off-the-hook kind of therapy.

In the US you have fifty minutes, and then the therapist might say, "Oh, it looks like we are out of time. Let's pick that up next week." Biological Decoding, at least what I experienced of it, was more like, "I see this topic is upsetting you. Good. Let's dive into that. Let's rearrange that memory into something positive. No matter how much you don't want to talk about it. Let's focus on it like a laser beam – let's make the traumatic thought something positive."

We did the deep dive into the darkest and most painful memories in THE BOX and I in fact passed out. Mission accomplished! Nico knew his stuff. Oddly enough, my passing out built trust. It didn't break it. I looked forward to the next session. Maybe this would actually be effective! Once again, I had hope.

The sessions were months apart and Nico warned me that my body would be processing the impurities that we dislodged from my subconscious mind and I may get sick - fatigued, diarrhea, headaches et cetera. All of that and more happened to me. Nico kept in contact with me through all of that. I was beginning to believe this could work.

Now, I didn't go into this blind. I read a book. I talked to Steve after every session with Nico just to check in and see if what was happening made sense. Steve was awesome. He'd say to me, "I can tell from what you're telling me and how you're describing things, Matt, that this is working for you. Keep doing it. And remember, you don't need to know why it's working or how it works. Just accept that it is working."

When Nico and I finished all of the sessions, he told me it may take a few months to see if what we worked on helped. A few months went by, and as it did, I knew it was working. My nightmares were fewer and farther between. I started racking up nights in a row nightmare-free. Over time, my daytime symptoms vanished.

At some point, Nico asked me if I had PTSD. I replied, "No, I don't have any symptoms of PTSD." I couldn't believe that came out of my mouth. I had made it! I climbed the mountain. I chose the hard paths at every turn. I chose to face my fears. I chose to step through anxiety. I chose to do whatever I needed to do to find a way to be healthy. And now, I am HEALTHY!

What I learned

Finding Nico was pure chance through Matias, and it worked out great for me, but here's what I learned about researching alternative therapies:

- *Ask practitioners about their training and credentials*
- *Request references from other patients (if they can share any)*
- *Understand the process before you start*
- *Nico explained everything upfront*
- *Have a support system in place*
- *Nico insisted I have someone nearby*
- *Research as much as you can, even when information is limited*
- *Trust your instincts about whether something feels right for you*

I always discussed new treatments with my established medical team (Steve and Adam) before trying them.

THE HARD WORK IN CHOOSING TO HEAL

It isn't easy to heal your mind, body and soul. You have to remember, look at and relive the darkest things you've experienced. What drives someone to say, "enough is enough"? What drives someone to push through to go from victim to survivor?

For me, I kept reminding myself how much of my life Rusty had stolen. The rest of my life was going to be mine! "Rusty doesn't get to win" became my mantra.

I remember Nico asking me, "Are you ready to heal?" I didn't understand at the time what he meant. Now, I do. When you are ready to heal and take back your life, a strength you didn't know you had will emerge. Oh, it won't be easy for sure. But, you will persevere and push through all the pain. Rusty took too much from my past. I was determined to take back my future.

When Steve first suggested I share my story, I was so worried about saying it out loud. What did it mean if I did? Would the person I shared with break my trust and tell my story? Would they share MY details without MY permission?

Over time, years in fact, I shared small parts of my story. Examples of what happened. As I did, I'd share different pieces with different people so I knew who I told and what I told them. And I would tell them that they were the only person that knew. Then I'd wait to see if I could trust them. Great example of hypervigilance! It was exhausting to keep track of all that!

Remember, having one of God's representatives on earth tell you he cares about you and that God thinks you're special only to be RAPED by the same person and God not intervening to stop it, is one of the worst forms of trust violations. It is a terrible abuse of their position of authority.

Even to this day, I refer to all my doctors by their first names. You may have noticed I've done that throughout this book. It keeps us equal. It helps me feel safer and empowers me. I don't do well with people who prefer to use a title rather than their first name. I handle it this way: a doctor says, "Hi Matt, I'm Dr. John Doe." I reply, "It is great to meet you John."

Not all medical providers need to know I have PTSD. But, I've had to share with medical providers on occasion that I have PTSD. Especially if I think I might be triggered by something during an appointment. Does the dentist need to know? Probably not. Does the urologist? Absolutely. Make sense?

A funny thing just happened recently; I had to tell my dentist, I had PTSD. Why? During a night terror, I dislocated something in my jaw. The first assumption from the hygienist was that I might be grinding my teeth. When my dentist came in, I knew he needed to know what really happened for him to treat me. I asked to speak with him alone.

He readily obliged. Once we were alone, I told him I had PTSD, the source, the night terrors and how it was related to my jaw. I cried. We hugged. I cried more. Then, we came up with a plan for my jaw. He couldn't have handled that conversation better. I'm sure he was surprised, but his humanity came through instantly. He's a really good guy. I'm thankful he is on my journey with me.

So, I guess you need to decide who needs to know and when. That's the cool thing about having PTSD. WHAT!?! Are you kidding me? There's something 'cool' about PTSD? I get ya! But, it is cool to know that you are in control of who you share it with, when and why. It's empowering. You are in control of something!

And if sharing with someone doesn't work out, that's okay too. You've learned more. You are stronger for choosing to be vulnerable. You know, sometimes things don't work out and that's okay. Here's one example that comes to mind...

Something else that can happen when you tell someone you have PTSD is that they may get uncomfortable. Not because you have PTSD per se, but they may have their own experiences or trauma that interfere in how they think about the topic or the source of the trauma. Maybe they have their own anxieties or experiences with someone who had behavioral health issues that impacted them in ways they don't or can't share.

This situation has only happened to me once. I didn't take it personally. I recognized that the individual likely had their own trauma or experiences along their journey that had nothing to do with me. The personal filter they use on the topic makes it uncomfortable for them. I get it. I respect it. And I know, it is their issue and not mine to solve.

In this case, the individual said to me that they had nightmares for a week after hearing my story and a few months later said they were uncomfortable around me. I understood it. I knew they had their own anxieties.

I simply responded, "I'm a good guy who happens to have PTSD. If you want to talk, feel free to reach out." He hasn't. But, I don't worry about it. It's his issue, not mine. I still say "hi" to him. And if he does reach out at some point, I'll take the call. And if this happens to you, take the high road; it's empowering. And be kind to the person, they are on their own journey.

Before and since, I've been exceptionally careful what I share about PTSD and with whom. In fact, thanks to Rusty, trust is something I don't give people willingly. And if I do and it is broken, I can struggle significantly. But I choose to continue to trust. Again, I'm trusting you with my story.

Okay, so that's the mental aspect. What about your body after trauma? One of most difficult things I've been challenged to reconnect with after what happened, is the ability to feel. Shutting down from feelings is a way of surviving the abuse, it is a bodily reflex. Your mind separates from your body when your body is trapped. Unfortunately, it continued long after the threat had gone. I struggled with this for decades. And I didn't or couldn't explain it. Even once I knew what was causing this, and how to recognize when it is happening, it is still hard or impossible to control to this very day.

There are different ways the body separates from the mind. I think a medical term for something like this is dissociative. The trouble with dissociation or repression is that you cannot desensitize to just one type of feeling without shutting off all feelings. At least that is true for me.

The traumatic memories and the sensations they evoke, are blocked off by your brain as it continually works to keep these sensations from the surface. The brain is protecting you. My layman term for it is - stoic. No big highs and no big lows.

The rational part of you can go to work, earn money, appreciate that your wife and children are loving people and that they care for you, but you've got nothing left to feel or appreciate that. I have no doubt that that inability to feel impacted our marriage.

I would show love by doing things for my family. I found it difficult to feel though. I knew I loved my wife and kids. But, I struggled to feel that love. It's unfortunate that our marriage ended before that part of my healing process improved.

After a lot of hard work, I began experimenting with how to feel and do so without causing anxiety. This is mentioned often in this book. Remember to take note each time I mentioned that a hug felt safe. Those moments were moments my soul was healing and my body was beginning to feel again.

Now, what about trusting people? I have had more times than I care to admit where people I trusted with either the knowledge that I had PTSD or even with part of my story, shared my information with others. This ended relationships. It is and remains unhealthy for me to have people in my life who violate my trust, especially on this topic.

Some people worked through those issues with me. They're human too, after all. They didn't mean to share, and wanted to rebuild the broken trust. Others shared with intent. With those people I ended up parting ways. I couldn't have people in my life who were unhealthy for me.

When I finally started talking in my forty's about what had happened, I didn't share much with people beyond doctors. And doctors didn't ask me questions that they thought might trigger me. I always thought people would look at me differently if they knew. There's that word again, 'different'.

And with the way I grew up, I was sure someone would say, "You were RAPED by a priest? You're a faggot." Remember, this all happened long before the pedophilia of the churches became very public and long before political correctness became a thing, let alone more openness to talk about mental health issues.

As I was saying, a significant violation of trust happened from someone I thought was a friend. The details are not important. What is important is that my trust with that person was shattered.

I was in therapy with Steve and I told him what happened. He wasn't pleased either. I said, and I meant it, "I'll never trust anyone with my information again!" Steve replied, "You've been talking about this new guy you know, and you seem to trust him a lot." I said, "Yeah. He is a great guy." Steve replied, "Tell him your story and we will talk about it next time."

I was pissed! I just said I'm not going to tell anybody else! Didn't Steve hear me?!? I should fire him for not listening! Then, I started to see what he was doing. He didn't want me to get stuck in an unhealthy spot. He wanted me to step through the trust violation.

So, I reached out to this new friend. I explained in general terms that I needed to share something with him that would be hard for me. We agreed to meet at the local Starbucks.

When we got there, we got coffee and sat down. I realized this was a bad idea. I couldn't talk about this in a public place. I needed to leave now! So, I started to make up an excuse to leave. But, instead, we decided to sit in one of our cars and talk there.

I told him two pieces of my story of being RAPED and they happened to be two of the hardest things I went through. Why I picked those two hard topics, I don't know. They just came out. It wasn't planned.

I was a blubbering mess. I was balling my eyes out. He listened intently. He was supportive and gave me room to share and grieve as I needed. We were there for about two hours.

After I regained my composure, with great trepidation I asked him, "Now that you know what happened to me, do you think differently about me?" He said, "Yes. I used to respect you. Now, I respect the hell out of you!" In that moment, that was exactly what I needed to hear and I know he meant it.

Later, I told him why I needed to tell him part of my story. I said, "I trusted someone and I should never have trusted them." He replied, "No.

You trusted him and it didn't work out. Sometimes in life that happens." He and I are still close friends. I appreciate and love him a great deal.

The next time I saw Steve, I told him that I chose to trust someone new despite what happened and how it went. He applauded my courage. And I think he even said, "I told you so." It made me laugh.

What I got out of that lesson is worthy of mentioning to you, reader. Life isn't linear. It doesn't always go the way we want. And when things go awry and they will, what matters is how we pick ourselves back up again. Maybe you can learn to trust again. You may need to walk away from someone that harmed you and that's okay. Sometimes it's the healthiest thing to do.

I could have chosen to never trust anyone ever again. That was an option. It still is and Steve knew it. And if I didn't trust ever again, where would I be?

For one thing, this book would have never been written. Why? Because now, I'm trusting all of you with my information. That is scary as shit and I think about it often as I write this, wondering if I'll ever publish this book.

If you're reading this, it's proof that I've continued challenging myself and trusting new people! I encourage you to do the same. This book was exceptionally difficult for me. Not only reliving my past, but knowing the intent was to once and for all share my truth. To shine light into the darkness. To stand on the mountaintop and yell to world, "I HAVE PTSD!" But once I've done that, the thought of it can't scare me anymore.

There is hope. You can be healthier than you are today. I know, I've done it. And let's be honest here - it is a journey. The path is not linear, but the trajectory is towards a healthy life. To go from surviving life to living it and feeling it!

A great book that I purchased read and re-read many times is, The Body Keeps the Score by Bessel van der Kolk. This book "traces the history of trauma therapy and describes the treatments often used." It will help you learn how trauma affects the body and encourage you, like I'm doing via this book, to be an active participant in your healing. You can't heal if you expect others to do the work for you. The people helping you on your journey are your guides - you are the one that will need to do the work. If you step through the anxiety and act - great healing awaits you!

What I learned

Practical steps for building your healing team:

- *Start with one person you trust completely (for me, initially that was Steve)*
- *Ask your trusted providers for referrals to others*
- *Interview potential new providers - most will do brief consultations*
- *Don't be afraid to "fire" providers who aren't the right fit*
- *Keep a list of your triggers and needs to share with new providers*
- *Build relationships slowly - trauma makes trust difficult, and that's okay*
- *Remember that your healing team might change over time as your needs evolve*

Building trust after trauma takes time. Be patient with yourself and don't settle for providers who don't make you feel safe.

CHAPTER 8

THE MOUNTAINTOP

TRIUMPH

Here I stand on the mountaintop! I'm enjoying the view and looking back at everything I've been through to get here. This is what it feels like to be healthy! This is what it's like to be free of the past! This is what it feels like to lug a boulder up a mountain, get to the top and set it down. Triumph!

I have told all my friends that helped me on my journey. Some cried. They had seen what I had been through, worried about me; some had taken the calls in the middle of the night. They had come to my house when I was suicidal or gone to some of my doctors' appointments when I was too anxious to go alone. This is their achievement too!

I celebrated when I reached the milestone of ten years since I was diagnosed with PTSD. Ten freaking years! Life is good! I was two years completely symptom-free from PTSD following Biological Decoding. TWO YEARS SYMPTOM FREE! Can you believe it? It is possible for you, too. I hope you reach that level of peace.

And life, like PTSD, isn't a linear path. In 2021 I blew out my knee riding a One Wheel electric skateboard. My brain reminded me that pain is connected to the past. PTSD symptoms returned. Since then I've dealt with knee surgery and even fell getting out of the shower once recently.

I recalled Steve saying to me many times, "Matt, you will always have PTSD. But, the goal is for the symptoms to be fewer and farther between and less intense."

Biological Decoding worked. All my efforts in therapy and physical therapy paid off. I had two years of normalcy from the past. At this point,

I have had symptoms return and I know there is more work to be done to heal my soul.

But, unlike when I started this journey, I now have objective and logical proof that there are ways to heal. And I have memories of the emotions and peace that came along with reaching that mountaintop. Nothing can take those away from me now that I have earned them.

Here's what I've learned about healing...I've learned to be touched in safe and healthy ways. I've gone from keeping male friends no closer to me than a handshake to actually hugging those friends and feeling safe doing it.

In fact, I joked with Steve once that I was going to learn to be a hugging machine. I was determined to hug my friends until they were uncomfortable! It was great humor!

I've learned to meditate. I've learned to share parts of my story. I've learned to trust. I've learned to recover from violations of trust. I've learned to ask for help. I've learned to be pragmatic about accepting help I didn't ask for when others see I'm in need of it.

I've learned to reach out to friends when suicidal ideations happen. I've learned that too much down time doesn't work for me. I've learned to keep a schedule - routine keeps me grounded. I've discovered being in nature is healing and relaxing.

I've learned PTSD can suck. But, having PTSD doesn't make someone crazy. I'm just a normal guy like everyone else; I just happen to have PTSD. I've lived and continue to live a normal, happy, and productive life that sometimes gets thrown off track at unpredictable times. I've learned to be okay with that when it happens.

I've even learned to forgive. I have forgiven Rusty. I didn't forgive him for his sake. I forgave him for mine. I also forgave those that violated my trust along the way. It's enlightening to have the power to forgive.

There's a reward I didn't know possible in forgiving. It takes a weight off you. It frees you from the past. It allows you to go from victim to survivor. It allows you to move forward unbound. It can help heal your soul.

I've learned to be open to new ideas. If I had never met Matias, I wouldn't have learned about Biological Decoding from his brother Nico.

I've learned not to fear what I don't understand, and that if something is working, to let it continue.

I've learned to be vulnerable with the people I choose to trust. To be real and raw. My chiropractor once said to me, "You have great people surrounding you, Matt. These people are with you because of who you are as a human being. You are one of the most genuine individuals I have met and others see that too."

I've learned that hiding in your house to avoid PTSD triggers isn't rational. As Steve reminded me more than once, "Matt, you can move to a mountain side, live in a yurt and raise some goats to avoid being triggered. But, is that the life you want to lead?"

So unfortunately, no, I have not healed my soul completely. But, I *am healing*. And I will continue to find ways to heal my soul. I've been symptom free in the past. So, I know I can get there again and so can you. What I won't do is stop trying and neither should you.

Two steps forward and one step back, is still one step forward. Every set back is an opportunity for a new success. And you won't lose what you've learned if what you try doesn't work. You've just learned more.

There are many things I chose not to put in this book. There are medical issues and therapies I'm working through at the time of writing. I've shared a lot more in these writings than I ever thought I would. I also learned that I don't need to share everything. That's true for you too. Pick and choose what works for you on your journey.

What happened to me doesn't define me. It is a part of me. And combined with all my other experiences, and my choices, it makes up who I am as a human being.

As shocking as it might sound, I wouldn't change anything that happened in my life. It is because of the collection of those events in my life that I am who I am. I am imperfect. I'm learning. I'm growing. I have an enormous empathy for others. I take care of and look out for people. I *like* me.

We are all works in progress. Learn to like yourself. In fact, love yourself! You are amazing, unique and flawed. Be kind to one another. Why? Because someone you interact with in your daily routine may have trauma you can't see, touch or feel. They may be trying to heal their soul too.

An act of kindness from you may get them out of their suicidal ideations. An act of kindness from you may help them feel like they matter. An act of kindness from you may be the thing they need to make it through their day. Wouldn't the world be a greater place with more kindness?

MY AWESOME AND
AMAZING LIFE

This book has been focused on what went wrong in my life and how I found ways to overcome it. In addition to my trauma, PTSD and the recovery along the way I also lived a normal life and sometimes had fantastic and privileged experiences.

I've had job changes, financial challenges, got married, had two amazing boys (adults now), and a divorce after nearly thirty years together. I'm thankful for every moment she and I spent together, the kids we raised, and that she and I are still part of each other's lives.

I've had friends and family die. I graduated from college twice. I was elected and reelected to the NH House of Representatives in my 20's where I fought for ethics in government. I've traveled in Europe, Central America, the Caribbean, the Middle East, Africa and Southern Asia.

I was selected by our state newspaper, the NH *Union Leader,* as one of the 'forty under 40' emerging leaders in NH. I worked for three NH Governors (both political parties) representing them in collective bargaining with state employees.

I've hiked in many of the US National Parks and many of the peaks in the White Mountain National Forest right here in beautiful New Hampshire. I've worked on and vacationed at my grandfather's old dairy farm in Vermont. There's actually a road named after him in East Burke, VT - Marshall Newland Road.

I've played Texas Hold'em. I loved coaching soccer and did so for fifteen plus years. I've gone to many concerts - David Lee Roth is my favorite entertainer. I love to go see action movies - especially in IMAX. I enjoy CrossFit and the people that make up that community.

I've learned to wake board. I've tried surfing in the ocean. I've scuba dived and gone deep sea fishing. I've ridden horses. Mountain biked. I've skydived. I found through experiences with my son that I like live musicals! I love to play Dungeons and Dragons. Oh and who can forget the board games Risk and Axis & Allies?!?

I'm fortunate that I'm still friends with the 'Heights Boys'. We still have to be thick-skinned around each other. And you guessed it, I've started hugging them. And that's new to all of us. I'll keep at it. They are a tough bunch.

And it may be unusual but it's true - I've never drank alcohol nor done drugs. NEVER! It deserves all caps. It's an accomplishment. I'm as clean as they come that way.

These are just a few of the things that are part of what makes up my life and my experiences. And there's a lot left I want to do. And even when PTSD symptoms surface, I don't just survive; I am determined to live my life. We only have one life after all!

Nothing has ever been more important to me than being Dad to my kids. Because without my kids, who would I tell dad jokes to? Am I right boys? Talking rabbits! (They'll know what I mean!)

SOME FINAL
THOUGHTS

Since that knee injury in 2021, I have had ups and downs. I had to accept I needed help. Talk about a triggering thought! I needed to trust someone with my care after two years symptom-free. It was humbling.

As word spread about my knee, my family, friends and my CrossFit community came to my aid. The vast majority of them didn't know I had PTSD. They didn't know I had been standing atop the mountain just the year before.

Then something started I also didn't expect. A few people with only the greatest of good intentions, who didn't know about my past, used this phrase when I was nearing knee surgery and after: "I'll keep you in my thoughts and prayers." Yes, "prayers."

I have tried on and off to have conversations about God and religion with different people. And once again, I'm so fortunate. I have people in my life who are willing to talk to me who happen to be varied in their belief systems: Catholic, Episcopal, Orthodox, Jewish, Pentecostal, Mormon, Jehovah's Witness, Christian, Spiritual, Agnostic, some who say they are not religious at all but have a relationship with Jesus, and Atheists amongst many others.

One of these people recently reached out to me after having met me only twice. He told me he found that I had a "gentle strength and a caring, giving and take-responsibility spirit." He said, "That's a different kind of strength most 'strong' men don't know how to show." Another time I mentioned to a new friend that I was thankful that I'm healthy enough to help others. He replied, "You truly are a gift to this world."

Hearing things like that makes me grateful for everything that has happened in my life. There is purpose in our lives, whether we are religious, believe in God or not. We all have a chance to impact people positively in small and big ways that may help them in their lives and along their journeys.

I know many people who sought out God at different points in their lives and doing so helped them lead better lives. It gave them purpose. For some, it helped them let go of addictions. I respect what religion and God can do for people. That, unfortunately, has not been my journey.

When I get angry hearing about child sex abuse in the church and elsewhere, sometimes I think, "My life makes more sense if God doesn't exist. And, if he does exist, I hate him." I get viscerally angry at the Bible thumpers. You know, those who use the Bible to discriminate against others who disagree with them. It infuriates me that two people can look in the same book, at the same verse even, and walk away with one showing grace and love and the second person claiming the first person is not only mistaken but their showing of grace and love is a sin or even evil.

It has become apparent to me that I've never dealt with how I feel about religion. My conversation with God (if he exists) ended when I was about twelve years old. I now recognize that this is going to be part of my journey down the mountain. I feel the need to reconcile the part that religion played in harming me, stealing my childhood, and raping my soul. Once I know how this journey down the mountain goes, maybe I'll write another book.

Oh! I also started a new to me therapy – EMDR.

Until then...

ACKNOWLEDGEMENTS

There are so many people in my life that have had a positive impact on me growing up and into adulthood before and during my journey with PTSD. I've mentioned many of them or referred to their actions in the book. They know who they are.

I was told for years to try journaling as part of a way to heal. I was told that thoughts going from the brain, down my arm, into my hand and out my fingers and then onto paper (or in this case an iPad) would somehow make me healthier. You've read my trauma. I never wanted that on paper - NEVER EVER!

I spent the summer of 2022 hiking on and off with a friend from the gym and we'd take along my son's dog Karl. He and I got to know each other pretty well.

One day he saw me have a panic attack at the gym. He followed me out to my truck. He didn't know my story at the time. As I was trying to calm down and stop crying, he suggested I try journaling to make sense of things.

Internally, I rolled my eyes. Like, "Yeah, you know how many times I've been told that?!? No way in hell am I going to put down in writing what happened to me."

Well, then I wrote this book. Go figure! For some reason hearing it again and from him made a difference. I wrote this book in nine days. The words poured out of me, and I am proud of my work.

And to the Heights Boys - well, there you have it! You may have learned something about me you didn't know. Now, get writing! I want to read *your* stories! There are people who could be healed by our journeys.

I am so fortunate to have had the greatest cast of wonderful and unique characters in my life who have been with me through thick and thin. Lifetime friends, friends who recently entered my life and some who have moved on. All of whom I'll always cherish with my imperfect mind and my healing soul. I wouldn't change a thing!

For those of you I may have left out of this book, know there's a reason. The things you shared with me while helping me heal, those are *your* stories. I am forever grateful for your kindness and willingness to be vulnerable right alongside me. Thank you for your willingness to trust me with your trauma and topics you've struggled to overcome. Our friendships are stronger and deeper because of it.

I choose to continue to respect and protect the things that you've shared and worked on with me to help me heal. And those will remain forever between you and I. Thank you for being you and being an important part of my life and my journey. I love you and I will be there for you just as you have been for me.

And to Alexis, who entered my life as I was putting the final touches on this book and deciding about its release - thank you for loving all of me, including the parts still healing.

OH, AND ONE
MORE THING

Throughout my healing journey, I struggled with whether to reach out to the church that employed Rusty. After years of therapy and growth, I finally found the strength to seek answers. In December 2019, I wrote to the bishop. What follows is that correspondence, shared here exactly as written.

I have written to the bishop where Rusty worked, and I have received a reply.

Actual Letter to the Bishop (Unedited)

December 10, 2019
Bishop Devadhar,
I read for the first time Matthew Treadwell's blog post about Rusty Pettis last year. I drafted this email to you shortly after reading Matt's post. But, I wasn't healthy enough to send it. So, I kept it in my draft folder and re-read it on and off until deciding to send it today.

I too, like Matt Treadwell, am a survivor of Rusty's abuse. My abuse at the hands of Rusty started in a very similar way as Matt's. An overnight church outing and a back rub. The abuse went on for about a year to a year and a half.

While I'm not going to write the details of my abuse in this email, I do want you to know a few things that are at the core of not only the physical abuse - but the mental torment. Rusty used God as his power base to control me in his physical abuse. 'Abuse' is too kind of a word actually – it's rape.

Not only was he a leader in the church, he would say things like, "It's God's will" and "A gift from God". He would threaten me and my family if I told anyone by saying things like "God is all knowing" implying Rusty would find out or God himself would punish me if I told anyone. He would get angry if I resisted. So, in the mind of a twelve year old, to keep me and my family safe, I never told an adult. He stole my childhood.

I survived most of my adult life by burying this information. Never dealing with it. My inability to process what happened caused me a lot of relationship issues; inability to trust, not getting too close to new people, anger, depression and a lot of other things that went along with that.

At around age forty, I had a lower back injury. When I began physical therapy, I started having episodes of passing out, anxiety and depression. When I was touched by the physical therapist(s), I also began having flash-backs to rape at the hands of Rusty. I couldn't process what was happening and I ended up hospitalized for over a week in July of 2010 and then out of work for six months to deal with what was diagnosed as Post Traumatic Stress Disorder (PTSD). PTSD will be with me for the rest of my life. At the height of PTSD I couldn't drive by a church (any church) without having a trigger, flashback or panic attack.

After being diagnosed with PTSD and heavily medicated via prescrip-tions at the time, about eight years ago or so, I walked into the Wesley United Methodist church offices on Clinton Street in Concord, NH and told my story or at least as much as I was able to say out loud. At that time, I was suffering every day/night from panic attacks, nightmares, flashbacks and/or night terrors. I told the individual that I was sharing with them be-cause I wanted to be able to sleep at night and I needed to know kids are safe.

He told me he went up the ranks of the Methodist church with Rusty and knew that there were rumors of Rusty's behavior. And that Rusty was no longer with the United Methodist Church. The last thing he told me is that he believed Rusty moved to Wyoming. He then brought me into the hallway that has all of the pictures of church leaders and walked me to Rusty's. I was numb. Numb is the only word I could use to describe seeing his photo. I wondered why it was even hanging on the wall. Was the church proud of him? If the church knew of the abuse, as I had just been told, why was the church spotlighting a pedophile? Why hadn't they taken the picture down?

Later, I was able to Google the "Rusty Wyoming" information and found that Rusty had worked at a church in Laramie, WY. Rusty had already left that church by the time I found it. From there, I found out that he was a counselor after leaving the church. I sent an email to his employer through their web page letting them know he was a pedophile, told them to keep him away from kids and urged them to contact the churches in NH he worked at to confirm it. It was the best I could do given my health issues at the time.

For years, I checked the obituaries in Laramie, WY regularly to see if he passed away. I was hoping that if he did, the nightmares and night terrors would end. I always told myself that when Rusty was dead I would be able to rest easy and sleep again. It was just over a year ago, that I found out Rusty had died by suicide through Matt Treadwell's blog. Unfortunately, the rest I hoped would happen hasn't happened that way for me. In fact, the symptoms of PTSD are at the forefront as if rape was happening all over again and likely will be so for months or longer as I process this new information. I'm only beginning to have one or two nights in a row without nightmares.

Just over three years ago, after nearly thirty (30) years together, my wife divorced me. She said that she finally understood why my past and the PTSD had impacted our relationship. But, by then it was too late.

This journey of healing for me is going to be ongoing for the rest of my life. PTSD is also with me for the rest of my life. The doctors have told me the medical hope is that the symptoms/triggers of PTSD will be fewer and farther apart and less intense as I continue to heal. But, PTSD will never go away.

I have no relationship with a church. Church and church leaders have been and continue to be a trigger for PTSD. The fact that after a decade of dealing with PTSD and the health struggles it creates, that I'm finally able to write this email to you, is a testament to everyone who has walked with me on this journey of healing and the strength of conviction I have in fighting to reclaim my soul from Rusty's abuse.

I have survived life, but, my goal is to live life fully. Reclaiming my soul, healing my soul, is how I will go from surviving life to living life. Reaching out to you is part of that healing process for me as I find my voice and try to heal my soul.

With the knowledge of Rusty's suicide, some of my first thoughts were that; I'll never be able to confront him; the adults in my life when I was a child failed me; people who knew the rumors failed to act; the church and its leaders failed to defend and protect children in their care.

Thanks to Matt Treadwell's blog post, I now know factually that I wasn't the only one raped at Rusty's hand under the power of the United Methodist Church and I'm sure that there are others. Just like the Catholic Church, the United Methodist Church can't continue to hide this. It's wrong to sweep it under the rug. Transparency is the only solution.

The right thing for the church to do is own it, shed a light on it, apologize for it publicly, reach out to those who have yet to come forward, make it right with those who were raped, and take concrete actions to ensure it isn't happening to anyone else now, and put processes in place that will ensure it will never happen again.

I have a simple question for you. What happened?

Matt
Matthew John Newland

ACTUAL RESPONSE FROM THE BISHOP (UNEDITED)

December 17, 2019

Dear Mr. Newland,

Greetings in the precious name of our Lord and Savior Jesus Christ.

Isaiah 41:10 says: "Fear not, for I am with you; be not dismayed, for I am your God; I will strengthen you, I will help you, I will uphold you with my righteous hand."

In difficult times, it is always good to remember that nothing can separate us from the love of God, and though we may face trials, none of them can overcome us as long as we remain in God's presence.

My heart breaks at receiving your email regarding the harm you suffered by Rusty Pettis. However, I am grateful for your courage in reaching out to me with your story. I want you to know that upon hearing the story first from Mr. Treadwell, we responded quickly to care for victims, to alert the Wesley community, and to ensure that Mr. Pettis would do no more harm.

Shortly after hearing from Mr. Treadwell, we met with his family and other members of Wesley UMC in Concord, as well as staff and volunteers from Wanakee Camp in Meredith, NH. We were able to confirm that Ernest Pettis was accused of sexual abuse of minor boys at the Canaan, VT church in the early 1980s and was subsequently removed from the church and asked to undergo psychiatric evaluation. When he refused to comply with the church's demands, Mr. Pettis was asked to surrender his credentials with The United Methodist Church, which became official July 5, 1983.

Upon receiving this information, we immediately notified Mr. Pettis' employers and local law enforcement in Wyoming. My episcopal associate, Rev. Erica Robinson-Johnson, read the attached disclosure letter at all the worship services at Wesley UMC in Concord as an attempt to bring information, healing and support for anyone else who may have been harmed by Mr. Pettis. Mr. Pettis' photograph was subsequently removed from the church hall.

I am so very sorry for the pain you have suffered and for any further pain caused you by The United Methodist Church. While I was not the Bishop at the time this happened, I can assure you that we do not tolerate any form of sexual harassment or abuse and take every allegation very seriously.

I know that this will not erase your pain, but I do hope that it will begin to bring some level of comfort to you to know that the church responded in the 1980s as best it could and has implemented serious measures to prevent further abuse. You will continue to be in my prayers for healing. If there is anything that we can do for you, please don't hesitate to let me know.

We know that in all things, God is with us. In times like these, it is especially comforting to know that we never walk alone.

In Christ's love,
Bishop Sudarshana Devadhar
Resident Bishop
New England Conference – United Methodist Church

~end~

RESOURCES FOR HEALING AND SUPPORT

Crisis Support - Get Help Now

If you're having thoughts of suicide or self-harm:
- **988 Suicide & Crisis Lifeline**: Call or text 988 (available 24/7)
- **Crisis Text Line**: Text HOME to 741741
- **National Suicide Prevention Lifeline**: 1-800-273-8255
- **Emergency**: Call 911 or go to your nearest emergency room

PTSD and Trauma Support

PTSD Foundation of America
- Website: ptsdusa.org
- Provides education, support, and resources for PTSD

National Center for PTSD (U.S. Department of Veterans Affairs)
- Website: ptsd.va.gov
- Comprehensive information about PTSD, even for non-veterans

International Society for Traumatic Stress Studies (ISTSS)
- Website: istss.org
- Find trauma-informed therapists and treatment information

Sexual Abuse Survivor Resources

RAINN (Rape, Abuse & Incest National Network)
- National Sexual Assault Hotline: 1-800-656-4673
- Website: rainn.org
- Online chat support available 24/7

1in6
- Website: 1in6.org
- Specifically for men who experienced sexual abuse
- Online support groups and resources

National Child Traumatic Stress Network
- Website: nctsn.org
- Resources for childhood trauma survivors

Finding Mental Health Professionals

Psychology Today
- Website: psychologytoday.com
- Search for therapists by location, specialty, and insurance
- Filter for trauma specialists and PTSD treatment

American Psychological Association
- Website: apa.org
- Psychologist locator tool
- Information about different types of therapy

National Alliance on Mental Illness (NAMI)
- Website: nami.org
- Local support groups and education programs
- Family support resources

Specialized Trauma Therapies

EMDR International Association
- Website: emdria.org
- Find EMDR (Eye Movement Desensitization and Reprocessing) therapists

Somatic Experiencing International
- Website: traumahealing.org
- Body-based trauma therapy practitioners

Books Mentioned in This Memoir

"The Body Keeps the Score" by Bessel van der Kolk
- Comprehensive guide to understanding trauma and recovery options

Support for Families and Friends

National Alliance on Mental Illness (NAMI) Family Support
- Website: nami.org/Support-Education/Support-Groups
- Support groups for families affected by mental health conditions

Crisis Text Line for Support People
- Text HELLO to 741741
- Support for those helping someone in crisis

Substance Abuse Resources

SAMHSA National Helpline
- 1-800-662-4357

- Treatment referral and information service (24/7)
- Website: usa.gov/substance-abuse

Religious/Spiritual Trauma Resources

Survivors Network of those Abused by Priests (SNAP)
- Website: snapnetwork.org
- Support for clergy abuse survivors

Physical Health Support

American Physical Therapy Association
- Website: apta.org
- Find trauma-informed physical therapists

International Association of Healthcare Practitioners
- Website: iahp.com
- Find trauma-informed bodywork professionals

Financial Assistance

National Endowment for Financial Education
- Website: nefe.org
- Free financial counseling resources

United Way
- Call 211 or visit 211.org
- Local resources for financial assistance, healthcare, and support services

Legal Resources

National Crime Victim Bar Association
- Website: victimbar.org
- Legal resources for crime victims

Legal Aid
- Website: lsc.gov
- Free legal assistance for those who qualify

Online Communities and Support

Reddit Communities (Use with caution - not professionally moderated)
- r/PTSD
- r/adultsurvivors
- r/CPTSD

7 Cups
- Website: 7cups.com
- Free emotional support and counseling

Important Notes About Getting Help

What to Look for in a Therapist:
- Experience with trauma and PTSD
- Uses evidence-based treatments (CBT, EMDR, etc.)
- Makes you feel safe and heard
- Respects your pace and boundaries

Red Flags to Avoid:
- Pushes you too fast
- Dismisses your concerns

- Doesn't respect boundaries
- Makes you feel judged or uncomfortable

Insurance and Payment:
- Many therapists offer sliding scale fees
- Employee Assistance Programs (EAP) often provide free sessions
- Some community mental health centers offer low-cost services
- Call your insurance to understand mental health benefits

Remember:
- Healing is not linear - there will be ups and downs
- You don't have to heal alone
- It's okay to try different therapists until you find the right fit
- Healing is possible, even when it doesn't feel that way

This resource list is for informational purposes only and does not replace professional medical advice. If you're experiencing a mental health emergency, please contact emergency services immediately.

Resources accurate as of 2025. Websites and phone numbers may change over time.

ABOUT THE
AUTHOR

Figure 1 – Matt Newland, Hidden Lake, Glacier National Park, Montana

Survivor

www.ingramcontent.com/pod-product-compliance
Lightning Source LLC
Chambersburg PA
CBHW031525120626
46545CB00005B/2014